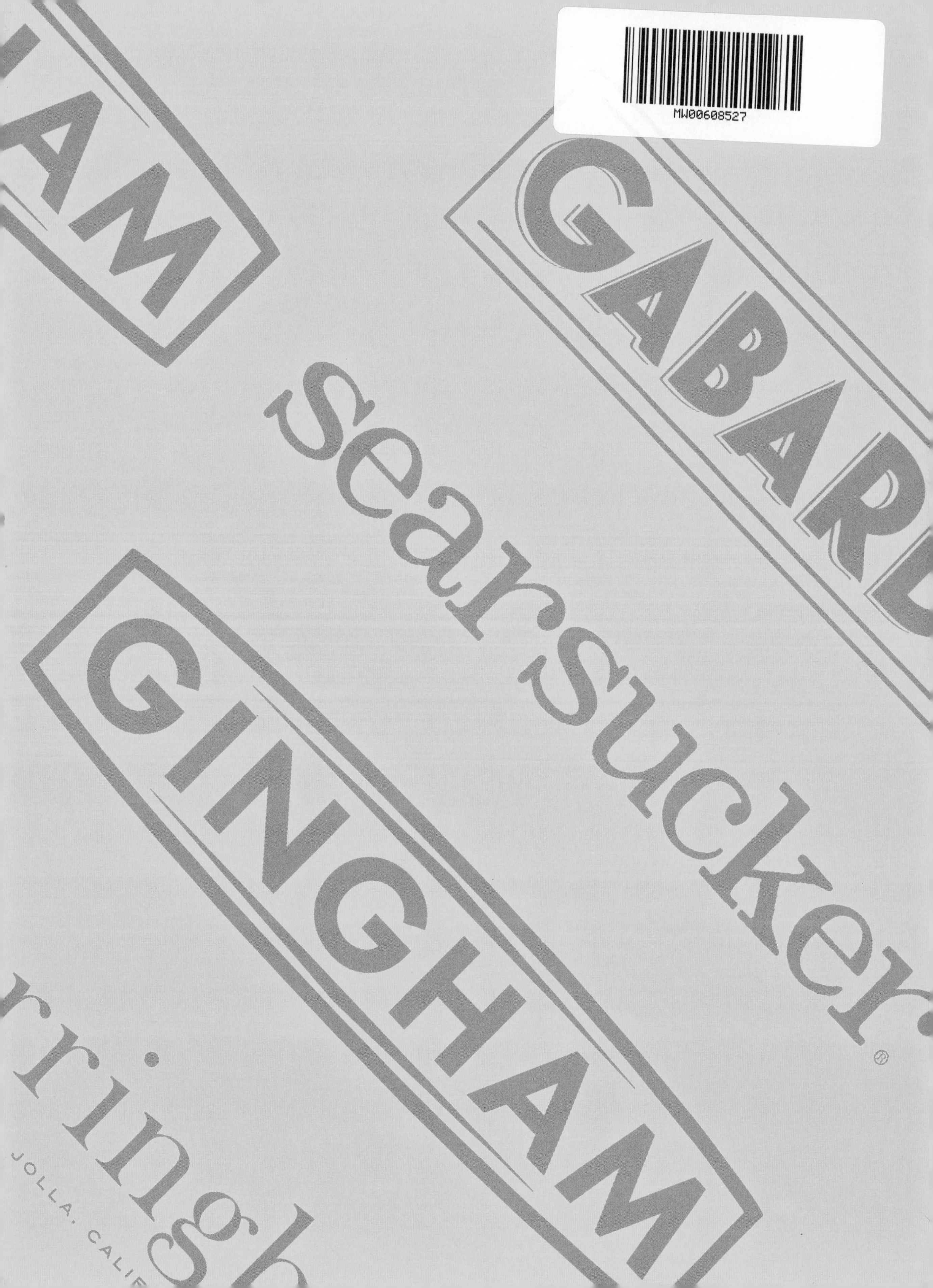
MW00608527
GABARD
searsucker®
GINGHAM

BRIAN MALARKEY

come early stay late

BRIAN MALARKEY

come early stay late

PHOTOGRAPHS BY MIKE PAWLENTY

San Diego, California

Published by Chefs Press, Inc., San Diego, California
www.chefspress.com

Publisher: Amy Stirnkorb
President & CEO: Bruce Glassman
Executive Vice President: Michael D. Pawlenty
Photography: Michael D. Pawlenty
Proofreaders: Margaret King and Lisa King

Chef's note: Many of the unique ingredients for Burlap's recipes are available at Asian markets, at specialty food stores, or online. In certain areas, even your local big-chain grocery stores (such as Ralphs, Albertsons, Vons, Kroger, Stop & Shop) may carry many specialty Asian ingredients.

Special Thanks to Chantelle/Hunter/Sailor/Miles/Stella Bleu — Daddy Loves U all so much!

ISBN: 978-0-9816222-7-9

First Edition
Printed in China

Food is not perfect. What we do in our kitchens, it has so many moving parts. The wine. The lights. The music. The chefs. The service. A million things can go wrong. And that's why it has to be said that our success is not about Brian Malarkey, it's about Team Malarkey. It's about all the incredible, dedicated, and talented people who make our restaurants great. The ones who facilitate your memories. It's a lot of people. And it's a big job. And there's no way one guy could even come close to doing it all. So, thank you. This book is for you.

inside

"This is how I cook. I'm the unapologetic Tong Chef — nearly everything I cook can be done with a pair of tongs."

THIS MAY BE THE ONLY COOKBOOK you'll ever read where the chef starts out by saying that food is not the most important part of eating. Yes, of course it's key, but this book is about everything else that goes into a great meal. It's not just about the ingredients and the directions that tell you how to make a recipe, this cookbook is about the adrenaline rush of cooking. It's about the rush of watching people eat what you cook for them. And it's about what food does for us socially. (Did you catch the subtle message to EAT that I put on the cover?) It's about the conversation. The laughter. Most of all, it's about food as fun! It's not what you prepare, it's how you prepare it and who you bring together.

So this is how I cook. I'm the unapologetic "Tong Chef"— nearly everything I cook can be done with a pair of tongs. Lots of chefs have their special collections of spoons, knives, eyedroppers, and instruments, but that stuff is not for me. I'm the king of the "one pan pickup." That means, I particularly love food you can do entirely with one sauté pan. Cooking this way, you can't micro-control everything that's going on in a dish. But I'm okay with the happy accident. I'm okay with the chaos. "Comfort in Chaos" is my mantra.

I don't care about food that looks really pretty. Yes, it should be appetizing. And yes it should be visually appealing. But I don't want to spend time building a tower or arranging every sprout of microgreens with a tweezer. And you know what? When you try too hard, when you try to work every little detail on a plate, you lose flavor (and heat!). I care about food that — when you put it in your mouth — you say "Wow! That tastes great!" So my advice: don't try to get elegant with the fried oysters, dude! Don't arrange them! Just toss them! Toss 'em in BBQ sauce and make 'em dirty! Make them taste great and that will make them fun. That's my style. As a chef, my main job is to facilitate your good time — the party.

It's easy, what we do. When you take away the pressure of a packed house for dinner on a Saturday night, the actual technique and approach to making our great dishes is simple. We take fresh, high-quality product, we season it well,

and we prepare it well. We don't make it more complicated than it needs to be. (Don't even get me started on molecular gastronomy! [Sorry Chef Sinsay] And yes, I know "molecular gastronomy" is just "revolutionary cuisine.") I don't put dots of sauce on a plate. I don't worry about the position of every grain of rice. And I don't send out plates that look like they've been touched by a dozen different people before they reach the customer.

When I put a plate down in front of a guest, I don't want to have a twenty-minute conversation about "sustainable" this, or "farm to table" that; or what position the harvest moon was in, or what the farmer's daughter's name was, or who milked the bull! I want my guests to look at what's on the plate, to smell it, to "eat it with their eyes" and to dig in. Enjoy! Does it taste good? Excellent! Then we have liftoff!

So, how did I arrive at my particular philosophy about food? Like most chefs, it has evolved over many years. It's a mix of both the positive and negative experiences I've had during my time in kitchens of all kinds.

I started cooking at home when I was just a young kid. My mom was a single parent in a little country town near Bend, Oregon, raising two kids on her own. She was really busy taking care of our animals (we lived on a 90-acre horse ranch) so I ate a whole lot of TV dinners. We left my dad when I was really young — he owned a roofing company and made shingles. I'm still convinced that the only reason my mom made her famous "Shit on a Shingle" for us, was as a not-so-veiled reference to my dad. Other than that, it was pretty much up to me to make stuff in the kitchen. So that's what I did. My mom would be out in the barn working in the stables at dinnertime, so I'd be in the kitchen, standing at the stove with my little pan. I can still remember one of my first dishes: rice with soy sauce and an egg on top. When I'd have a babysitter over, I'd be especially rebellious. When I first realized that my mom had turned my pet cow into the beef in our freezer, I exacted my revenge. I climbed up and pulled all the filets out of the freezer, cooked 'em up, and shouted "Yeah! Let's party!" (Those of you who know me may recognize a bit of that mischievous little brat that still remains…)

After basically failing out of the University of Portland as a business major, I went to Santa Barbara City College to study history and theater arts, which I loved. My dad came down and saw me in a play at one point and I remember he took me aside and said "Kid, you gotta get another job. You suck as an actor." Well, I gotta thank him for that. Turns out he was right. So I went to culinary school. I enrolled at Western Culinary Institute in Portland (now accredited as Le Cordon Bleu) but there was one problem: I hated it. I couldn't do the whole checkered pants, crevatte, and paper hat thing. So I didn't do very well at all.

It just so happened that my friend Henry Miller, who was on the culinary Olympic team, called me and told me he didn't really have the money to do an internship he was offered at Citrus in L.A. He told me I should go do it. So, I went down there, walked in, and I was blown away by it. It was the most gorgeous kitchen I had ever seen! "Lifestyles of the Rich & Famous" gorgeous (literally). And the executive chef, my first real mentor, Michel Richard, he was amazing. His food was like a magic trick. Precision and flawless technique. My job, for 6 weeks, was basically the shit work. I spent mornings turning artichokes and afternoons peeling asparagus. That was it. Not glamorous, but I put in my time. I got yelled at. I had spoons thrown at me. Worked sixty hours a week, and got paid for forty. But I realized this was a place for me. The teamwork was exciting. It was a thrill putting together beautiful food that went out to L.A.'s glitterati. It smelled good. And I felt good being there. Within eight months, I was roundsman (just below the sous chef) and I was in the big-time. I worked on my days off. I stayed late. I learned. I learned everything. And this was the first time in my life that I knew what I wanted to do. This was where I belonged. (I actually remember telling myself that, one day, I'm going to be able to say I came to Hollywood through the back door!)

After two years or so of the high-pressure and heavy-partying L.A. lifestyle, I was totally fried. Out of the blue, my uncle calls me. He's a track photographer (best in the biz) who shoots Churchill Downs and the Derby, and he asked me if I wanted to go to Minnesota to take photos of the races. Sure! Why not? He gave me an office, an assistant, an apartment, and more money than I'd ever seen before. So I was taking photos, but that was only on Thursday through Sunday. I needed something else. Something cooking-related. I needed the challenge of a professional kitchen. (I love a good challenge!) Cooking professionally, you get challenged every single night, and that

fuels me. So I decided I would walk into my favorite café in Minneapolis — the Loring Café — which was a beautiful, funky place; no uniforms, just a sexy, casual vibe. I walked in and I basically said "Hey, I'm new in town and I'd like to cook for you a few days a week." Yeah, right. "Who the f**k are you?" They looked at me like I had three heads. Then I told them I'd come from Citrus. Boom. Hired. And that was where I met my second major mentor, Stephen Brown. He was the real deal: a perfectionist who prized discipline, order, passion, and procedure. The food was casual, but the attitude was not! Today, he's considered the Godfather of the modern Minneapolis food scene (which is incredible!).

When my Minnesota gig was up, I had enough money to take my friend Henry Miller to Europe for three months. We backpacked everywhere, cooked in restaurants, ate on the docks, slept on the beach. We traveled to thirteen countries — including Spain, Italy, Morocco, and France — we shopped for food, and cooked for people in every country. I tasted my first really great tomato in Italy. And I came home from Europe with a new understanding of how to get out of the way of really great ingredients. I learned the art of not doing too much.

When I got back to the States, my girlfriend at the time, Chantelle (now my wife), convinced me we should move to Seattle so I could work for Oceanaire. It sounded like a plan, so we did it. I wound up working with Kevin Davis, who became another big mentor of mine. In the kitchen, Kevin was a highly driven, often abrasive, and demanding taskmaster. It wasn't all cherries and smoked almonds, but I learned a lot from him. Eventually, I took more of leadership position in the organization and I was offered the chance to open an Oceanaire in San Diego. I was 30 years old and they were offering me a chef-partner position! I took it! And, even better, I hired Mike Mitchell to join me in the front of the house. He also taught me a lot, and together we were unstoppable. We totally killed it. Oceanaire San Diego was a smashing success!

Fast forward to a San Diego Liver Foundation Gala I was cooking for, where I got into a balls-out competition with another chef who had been talking shit and egging me on. So I brought it. (I love a good challenge!) Went all out; some might say a little over the top. Let's just say I was wearing a giant lion's head, I had a team of servers with flames on their fingertips, and I nearly set the ballroom at the Omni ablaze. The guests were kicking and screaming with delight and amazement. The hotel and the Liver Foundation? They kicked me out.

Within a week or so of my three-ring Omni circus act, I got a call from the producers at "Top Chef." Turned out they had heard about my performance and they wanted me (I hadn't even put in an application). Right there everything changed.

People ask me about "Top Chef" more than anything else. It was obviously one of the most important things that has ever happened to me (seems like a hundred years ago now), not only because of the exposure, but also because of what I learned about cooking. I really learned some important lessons, like the pitfalls of overdoing a dish — of trying to do too many things on the same plate. I went way over the top in the first episode (snake AND eel!) and almost got kicked off right then and there (I was trying really hard to impress Anthony Bourdain and the others). It took some getting used to, especially with all the cameras, the lights, and the production people all over the place. It was a trial by fire.

The one thing about "Top Chef" that most people don't know is that — while the show brought me recognition and celebrity — it also gave me the confidence (and the thick skin) I needed to move my career forward. The show had 4 to 5 million viewers, there were articles, posts, and blogs from thousands of people all over the world, and some of those people were not fans. Some viewers were writing really nasty stuff about me, how I should have been kicked off, how they hated me — and it hurt at first. But that's when the skin develops. I realized I'm never going to have everybody love me. As soon as I accepted that, I didn't really care what anyone else thought anymore. I knew I was good, and I became much more confident about the idea of putting myself out there. It's best to make fun of yourself, to have the humility to laugh at yourself, to have fun and enjoy life. That's how you take the wind out of the naysayers' sails! And the people that don't like me? I'm okay with that. I'm me. And I'm doing what I want to do.

When the time came to think about my own restaurant, I had to do a lot of soul-searching. I had to figure out who I wanted to be as a chef and what kind of place would allow me to be that kind of chef. I thought a lot about Mario Batali (my idol). I love his food. It's simple. Clean. And he doesn't care what other people think. He's always done his own thing, no matter what. (I've been lucky enough to meet Mario. He once made a point of telling me that his kids love me. That was a defining moment in my life! I was young, I was insecure, and all of a sudden one of my idols said, "you're playing on my level." That just rocked me!)

I went headlong into the Searsucker project with everything I had. Worked literally night and day for months to make it happen. My good friend (and now business partner) James Brennan made sure we got the best of the best and — seemingly overnight — I went from simple chef to being a "restaurateur." What I blogged in the months before Searsucker opened, still remains true today:

I can guarantee one thing for sure and that is it will be an incredible play performed in the public eye with lots of story lines, hopefully seasoned with comedy, with a dash of drama and, of course, served up with lots of love. A true love story straight from my heart!

My goal is to stay true to this idea. To make sure Searsucker and the other restaurants don't lose sight of the basic principle: We're trying to be mainstream. Our goal is to feed lots of friends. We want to make food that we're proud of, that we love, and that makes people happy and feel good. We're not struggling artists, not the misunderstood geniuses who want to teach the world how to eat...We want to feed the people. Not the elites. Not the snobs. We don't cater to those guys that come in, get their food, and immediately start Yelping and Tweeting and blogging. I look at them and I think to myself, "Dude, you missed it. The entire point. You totally missed it. Be Here Now!"

I'm trying hard not to "miss it," too. I'm at a time in my life (speeding headlong into my forties — gulp!) where I feel like I should be on top of the world, but I actually feel like I have more challenges now than ever before. And more reasons to prove myself. I'm not content with standing still. But I am confident.

So, this attitude, this sense of well-being, this confidence (whatever you want to call it) is at the center of every recipe on these pages. It's what my book is all about. It's about a guy who's come to a point in his life and career where he can say — to himself and others — relax. Don't take things so seriously. Food isn't serious. Food is about more than eating the stuff on your plate; it's about the conversation, the laughter, and the memories. Food brings us together. It's the medium.

I hope you have a place where you can hang out with your friends, eat great food, listen to great music, and stay for hours just having a great time. I hope you have a place where you can come early and stay late, because that's what's it's all about.

sears

ucker

PEOPLE ARE ALWAYS ASKING ME ABOUT HOW THE NAME FOR SEARSUCKER came about, so here it is: It was post-"Top Chef," and my good friend James Brennan and I decided to start a restaurant together. James, who's a business-boy-genius, scored the best location in downtown San Diego. We got 7,500 square feet on the corner of Fifth and Market, the hub of the Gaslamp Quarter. I wanted the restaurant to focus on "new American classics," meaning that you take something familiar and you reinvent it. Playful tongue in cheek, the kind of place that — as soon as you walk into it — you let your guard down, you relax and enjoy being there. Restaurant names that had inspired me were The Village Idiot, Employees Only, Closed for Business, Father's Office; I needed something that just screamed "casual fun." So I was driving past the Del Mar Racetrack with my wife, Chantelle, and I was complaining that I wasn't going to have a chance to wear my seersucker suit to Opening Day, and I could see the light bulb go on over Chantelle's head. "Wouldn't that be a great name for the restaurant?" she said. We kind of laughed about it, but when I thought some more about it the name started to grow on me. When I Googled it, I found out that the word *seersucker* derives from a Hindu word meaning "milk and sugar," referring to the way that it ripples, like fabric. Then I learned that seersucker was worn by working-class people in the 1800s because it could be ruffled, it didn't have to be ironed, and you could stuff it in a knapsack and carry it around. Later in the 1800s, upper-class college and university kids all rebelled against their parents by wearing seersucker suits, which appalled the parents but made seersucker the "new vogue" and forever the summer fashion. Well, that's exactly what we wanted to do with our restaurant. We wanted people to be able to feel like they're dressed up in their comfortable seersucker suits, they're relaxed, feeling good, like they're taking a little summer vacation (it's always summer in San Diego). Thomas Schoos added the couches, right in the middle of everything (brilliant!) and James added the DJ and the music. It was great. And then I realized, on top of everything else, if I could put the word *suck* in the middle of our name and pull it off, that would really say something! And so, Searsucker and the whole "social dining experience" was born.

Chef Shane McIntyre

I was the first chef at Searsucker. It was my first restaurant, and I spent endless hours in there night and day, seven days a week. When it was time to start expanding, I had to be out a lot more, so I grabbed a very talented young chef named Shane McIntyre to become my five-star general on the field of battle. Shane came from a great restaurant group, and he was able to take my vision and really streamline it and really evolve it. He came in and worked my dishes inside and out, he got to really know my style, and he gained a true understanding of how we want to be playful and have fun. Shane is a natural leader in the kitchen, and he and the team have just done a great job keeping the vision and style of Searsucker exactly where it should be.

habanero pickles

serves 2 to 4 friends | as an app or side

When we were first putting together the menu at Searsucker, I wanted to have some really easy, inexpensive finger food, and I thought pickles. But I'm not the kind of guy that makes just an average pickle; I wanted to make a pickle that you'd remember for the rest of your life!

- 2 cups distilled white vinegar
- 1½ cups water
- 1½ cups granulated sugar
- 3 cloves fresh garlic
- 1 tablespoon black garlic
- 1 tablespoon coriander seeds
- 3 habanero chiles, cut in half (don't handle these babies without gloves — you'll regret it if you do!)
- 4 baby cucumbers
- Sea salt, to taste

[how to do it]

Chef's note: Black garlic is a fermented garlic that has a unique sweet-savory flavor. It is available at some supermarkets, at other specialty produce markets, or online.

1. Combine all the ingredients, except cucumbers and salt, in a medium pot and bring to a boil.
2. Lower the heat to a simmer and cook for 5 minutes.
3. Put the cucumbers in a clean glass container and pour the warm liquid over them to cover. Make sure the cucumbers are completely submerged. Store covered and refrigerated for a minimum of 3 days before eating, but try to be more patient. They will last up to a month and will only get better the longer you let them sit!
4. **To serve:** Slice the pickles on a bias and serve with a sprinkle of high-quality sea salt — at Searsucker we love to use Maldon sea salt.

"The Tabasco caviar is one of the coolest things we do at Searsucker. Chef Shane came up with the technique and people love it. Give it a try. Your guests will freak with delight!"

crab cakes + tabasco 'caviar' + tarragon aioli

serves 4 friends | as an app

I come from a long line of crab cake makers — and I've made many a crab cake in my day. I thought it would be fun to have a carb-free crab cake, so we've skipped the bread crumbs. Just straight-up crab. I love to do these in muffin pans at home — make them up, pop them in the fridge, and when your friends come over, toss them in the oven at 350°F and you're done.

[for the tabasco "caviar"]
½ cup water
½ cup Tabasco sauce
1 tablespoon agar agar
7 sheets gelatin, bloomed or softened in ice water
1 pint very cold canola oil (chill in the freezer for 3 hours)

[for the tarragon aioli]
1 cup mayonnaise
1 tablespoon freshly squeezed lemon juice
⅛ cup fresh tarragon, minced
Kosher salt and freshly ground black pepper, to taste

[for the crab cakes]
4 tablespoons mayonnaise
4 eggs
2 tablespoons freshly squeezed lemon juice
4 teaspoons Worcestershire sauce
Kosher salt and freshly ground black pepper, to taste
2 pounds whole fresh crab (whatever's in season and local, if you can get it), steamed or boiled and cooled

[finishing touches]
Fresh chives, roughly chopped
Lemon wedges, grilled

[how to do it]

Chef's note: Agar is a type of Japanese gelatin. It is available at Asian markets, online at willpowder.net, or from specialty food sources.

1. Make the caviar: Put the water and Tabasco into a pot with the agar agar and bring it to a boil. Take the pot off the heat and add the bloomed gelatin.
2. Take an eyedropper and drop the Tabasco mix into the cold oil. When all the Tabasco is in the oil, strain away the remaining oil and you will have Tabasco caviar!
3. Make the aioli: In a small bowl, whisk together all the ingredients and refrigerate until ready to serve.
4. Preheat oven to 350°F.
5. Make the crab cakes: In a medium bowl, combine the mayonnaise, eggs, lemon juice, Worcestershire sauce, and salt and pepper.
6. Open up the crabs, clean them out, and fold the meat gently into the wet mix (you don't want to break up the crab too much). Form the mixture into 4 patties (or use a ring mold if you want to get fancy) and lay them out on an oiled sheet pan.
7. Cook them in the oven for about 10 to 12 minutes, until they begin to get a light golden brown.
8. To serve: Place a crab cake in the center of each plate and top with the aioli. Add a nice spoonful of caviar, and garnish with fresh chives and grilled lemon wedges.

charred jalapeño tuna ceviche

serves 4 friends | as an app

I gave Chef Shane a challenge at Searsucker one day. I asked him to reinvent our original Tuna Poke and he came up with this great recipe. He uses charred jalapeños, which give an incredible spice and smokiness to the dish, and he uses only the freshest albacore (tombo). The recipe is simple, the presentation can be as fancy or casual as you like. No matter what, you'll love the flavors. Cold beer or sauv blanc makes it all perfect!

[for the tomato jam]
1 cup granulated sugar
1 cup Champagne vinegar
5 Roma tomatoes, diced small
½ yellow onion, diced small

[for the vinaigrette]
6 jalapeño chiles
1 cup water
1 cup Champagne vinegar
4 tablespoons honey
Kosher salt and freshly ground black pepper, to taste

[for the ceviche]
1 pound tombo tuna
1 tablespoon jalapeño chiles, seeded and minced
1 tablespoon fresh cilantro, minced
Kosher salt, to taste

[finishing touch]
Charred jalapeño chile

[how to do it]

1. Preheat a grill or oven to 400°F.
2. Make the tomato jam: In a medium saucepot, combine the sugar and vinegar and bring to a boil. Reduce the liquid by half, or until it's thick enough to coat the back of a spoon. Add the tomatoes and onion, bring the liquid back to a slow boil, and allow it to reduce for about 15 to 20 minutes, to a thick jam-like consistency. Cool completely.
3. Make the vinaigrette: Char the jalapeños either on a grill or rubbed with oil in a 400°F oven for 15 minutes. Cut the peppers in half and remove the seeds.
4. Put the charred jalapeños and wet ingredients into a blender and process until smooth. Season with salt and pepper.
5. Assemble the ceviche: Cut the tuna into very small cubes. Add the minced jalapeños, cilantro, salt, and vinaigrette to the level of spiciness you like. Let the tuna mixture marinate in the refrigerator for 1 hour. Taste and adjust seasoning if necessary before serving with the tomato jam. Garnish with additional charred jalapeño, if desired.

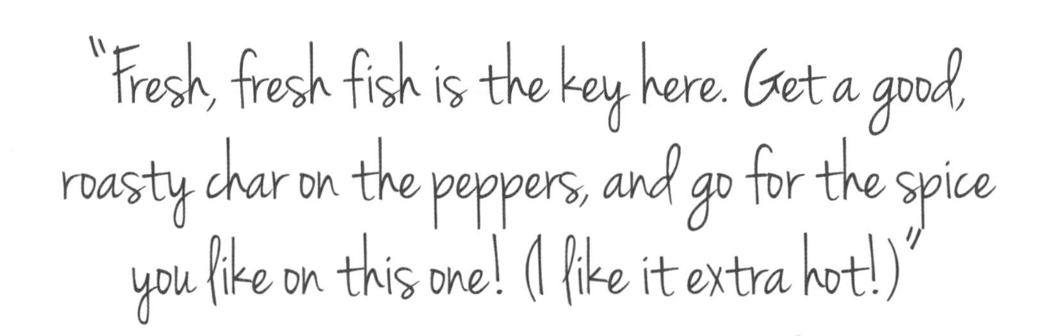

farm bird lollipops + snakebite hot sauce

serves 4 friends | as an app

When we first opened Searsucker, we had spicy chicken wings on the menu. People loved them, but we got lots of complaints that they were too messy. (Searsucker is a great date spot, but spicy chicken-wing fingers brings new meaning to the term "hot date!") So I asked super-chef Shane to reinvent the chicken wing. He came up with his from-scratch chicken chorizo and he put it on the end of a stick — voila! Fun, unique, spicy, and perfect for the hygienically challenged!

[for the chicken chorizo]
2 pounds chicken thigh meat, ground
4 tablespoons fresh garlic, minced
2 tablespoons paprika
2 teaspoons onion powder
2 teaspoons ground cumin
2 tablespoons kosher salt
1 tablespoon freshly ground black pepper
16 to 20 small wooden skewers

[for the blue cheese dipping sauce]
2 cups heavy cream
1 cup blue cheese, crumbled
2 tablespoons red wine vinegar
1 tablespoon Worcestershire sauce
Kosher salt and freshly ground black pepper, to taste

[for the snakebite hot sauce]
4 habanero chiles, diced
4 serrano chiles, diced
2 tablespoons olive oil
½ medium yellow onion, diced small
½ teaspoon cumin powder
½ teaspoon mustard seed
½ teaspoon cayenne powder
½ teaspoon paprika
½ teaspoon fennel seed
2 teaspoons chipotle chiles in adobo
1 clove fresh garlic
2 cups white balsamic vinegar
2 cups granulated sugar
3 cups piquillo peppers, diced

[finishing touches]
1 to 2 cups canola or vegetable oil, for frying
2 cups all-purpose flour, seasoned with kosher salt and freshly ground black pepper
2 cups blue cheese, crumbled
Fresh chives, minced

[how to do it]

Chef's notes: Piquillos are sweet Spanish peppers and are available at specialty food sources or online or you can substitute roasted red peppers. Also, your local butcher will be happy to grind up the chicken thighs for you.

1. Preheat oven to 350°F.
2. Make the chorizo: In a large bowl, combine all ingredients well. With an ice cream scoop or spoon, portion the chicken into balls and place on an oiled sheet tray. Skewer each chicken pop and bake for 10 minutes.
3. Make the dipping sauce: In a medium saucepot, bring the cream to a boil and remove from the heat. Whisk in all the other ingredients. Stir well to melt the cheese and combine. Allow to cool a bit, then refrigerate until needed.
4. Make the hot sauce: Sauté the habaneros and serranos in the oil until they become aromatic, about 5 minutes. Add all the remaining ingredients (except for the piquillos) and bring the mixture to a boil. Reduce the heat and simmer for 10 minutes to incorporate all the flavors. Take the sauce off the heat and stir in the piquillo peppers. Season with salt and pepper, to taste. In a blender, purée until smooth, and set aside.
5. Assemble the lollipops: In a deep fryer or medium skillet, heat the oil to hot (almost smoking). Roll the cooked chicken pops in the seasoned flour and fry until golden brown. Drain on paper towels.
6. To serve: Dip the fried chicken pops into the hot sauce, sprinkle with blue cheese crumbles and fresh chives, and serve immediately with dipping sauce on the side.

mushrooms + burrata on french toast

serves 2 friends | as a main

Okay, so this is the fun of this dish: Go to your local farmers market or favorite store and just pick out a boatload of mushrooms — any ones you like, the more the merrier. In this recipe, the mushrooms should show off a spectacular meatiness, and with the truffle oil, it's an intense mix of flavors. The burrata brings lightness and brightness to the earthiness of the mushrooms, and the French toast just sucks up all the flavors on the plate — as you will when you taste it!

[for the mushroom mix]
1 to 2 tablespoons canola oil
¼ pound beech mushrooms, sliced
¼ pound shiitake mushrooms, sliced
¼ pound cremini mushrooms, sliced
1 tablespoon fresh garlic, finely minced
1 tablespoon shallot, finely minced
½ teaspoon fresh thyme, finely minced

[for the french toast]
4 eggs
1 teaspoon Worcestershire sauce
1 teaspoon soy sauce
1 teaspoon Tabasco sauce
2 pieces thick-cut brioche bread ("Texas toast" size)
Butter, for frying

[finishing touches]
½ cup fresh burrata cheese or fresh mozzarella
Truffle oil
Fresh chives, minced

[how to do it]

1. Make the mushroom mix: In a very hot sauté pan, heat the oil and sauté the mushrooms until they start to brown and give up all their moisture (hot! hot! hot! is what you want). Add the garlic, shallot, and thyme and sauté until fragrant. Remove from the heat and keep warm.
2. Make the French toast: In a medium bowl, whisk together the eggs, Worcestershire, soy sauce, and Tabasco. Soak the brioche bread in the mixture for 30 seconds on each side.
3. In a medium-large sauté pan, melt the butter on medium-high heat and cook the toast pieces until both sides are golden brown.
4. To serve: Put each piece of toast in the center of a plate and top each with the mushroom mix. Garnish with fresh burrata cheese, a drizzle of truffle oil, and chives.

"This is a dish with real personality — great with a glass of red wine or rich, malty beer. It's one of our bestsellers at Searsucker."

prosciutto mozzarella salad

serves 4 friends | as an app

Super simple, super classic. Quick and easy to prepare. This one is all about the freshest ingredients and a simple, clean preparation that doesn't get in the way of the great flavors of the tomatoes, arugula, cheese, and prosciutto. Who says great dishes need to be complicated?

[for the pesto]
1 bunch fresh Italian parsley
4 leaves fresh basil
3 cloves fresh garlic
Kosher salt and freshly ground black pepper, to taste
1 cup olive oil

[for the lemon vinaigrette]
1 cup Champagne vinegar
1 cup freshly squeezed lemon juice
1 medium shallot, minced
2 cups canola oil
Kosher salt and freshly ground black pepper, to taste

[for the balsamic drizzle]
1 cup balsamic vinegar
1 cup granulated sugar

[for the salad]
6 cups (4 ounces) arugula
8 cherry tomatoes, cut in half
4 ounces fresh baby mozzarella, sliced
4 thin slices prosciutto
Kosher salt and freshly ground black pepper, to taste

[how to do it]

1. Make the pesto: In a blender, combine all the ingredients (except for the oil) on medium speed. When the ingredients are well combined, add the oil in a slow, steady stream to incorporate. Taste and adjust seasoning if necessary.
2. Make the vinaigrette: In a blender, combine the vinegar, lemon juice, and shallot. On medium speed, add the canola oil in a slow, steady stream to incorporate. Season to taste with salt and pepper.
3. Make the balsamic drizzle: In a small saucepot, combine the vinegar and sugar and reduce by half, until the liquid begins to thicken. Remove from heat and set aside to cool.
4. Assemble the salad: In a medium bowl, toss together the arugula, tomatoes, and mozzarella with some of the lemon vinaigrette and pesto, to taste. (Don't overdress your arugula. You can always add more, but light is best.)
5. To serve: Lay one slice of prosciutto on each plate and top with a portion of the arugula salad. Finish each plate with a drizzle of balsamic. Season with salt and freshly ground pepper, to taste.

strawberry summer salad

serves 4 friends | as an app

Every restaurant needs at least one salad that EVERYONE will love — this is that salad when the weather turns hot. It just screams SUMMER, and people love it for its classic mix of sweet, tart, savory, and salty. Remember to keep this one light — don't overdress it. Summer is all about wearing as little as possible!

[for the candied walnuts]
2 egg whites
1 to 2 cups whole walnuts, shelled
1 cup granulated sugar
1 teaspoon cayenne powder

[for the balsamic drizzle]
1 cup balsamic vinegar
1 cup granulated sugar

[for the champagne vinaigrette]
1 cup Champagne vinegar
1 tablespoon Dijon mustard
1 clove fresh garlic, minced
1 teaspoon shallot, minced
1 teaspoon fresh thyme, minced
1½ cups olive or canola oil

[for the salad]
2 nice big handfuls (about 8 ounces) mixed baby greens
12 strawberries, each cut into quarters
4 tablespoons goat cheese, crumbled
Kosher salt and freshly ground black pepper, to taste

[how to do it]

1. Preheat oven to 350°F.
2. **Make the candied walnuts:** In a medium bowl or mixer, whip the egg whites until frothy (1 to 2 minutes on medium speed). Add the walnuts and gently mix to coat. In a medium bowl, combine the sugar and cayenne, and mix well. Remove the walnuts from the egg whites and toss them with the sugar and cayenne. Spread the nuts on a sheet tray and toast in the oven until golden brown, about 12 to 15 minutes. Allow to cool.
3. **Make the balsamic drizzle:** In a small saucepot, combine the vinegar and sugar and reduce by half, until the liquid begins to thicken. Remove from heat and set aside.
4. **Make the vinaigrette:** In a blender, combine all the ingredients (except for the oil) on medium speed. Add the oil in a slow, steady stream to incorporate.
5. **Assemble the salad:** In a medium bowl, toss together all of the ingredients and mix with some of the vinaigrette. Taste to adjust dressing and season with salt and pepper. Toss in the walnuts (or top each plate with them) and finish with a healthy drizzle of balsamic.

"Put a big ol' platter of this salad out in the middle of the picnic table or by the pool, pour the sauvignon blanc, and everybody dig in!"

tombo + balsamic reduction + pesto

serves 2 friends | as an app

Here's a recipe that combines two of my favorite things: Fish and pork. There's nothing more tender or delicious than a great piece of fresh-cut tombo (albacore). And how do you make it even better? Wrap it in prosciutto! Dress it up with a little Euro-Italian influence (pesto and balsamic) and — bada-bing! — you've got "amore."

[for the pesto]
1 bunch fresh Italian parsley
4 leaves fresh basil
3 cloves fresh garlic
Kosher salt and freshly ground black pepper, to taste
1 cup olive oil

[for the tombo]
4 thin slices prosciutto
2 (8-ounce) pieces tombo, block cut
1 tablespoon canola oil

[for the balsamic reduction]
2 cups balsamic vinegar
1 cup granulated sugar

[finishing touches]
Edible flowers
Microgreens

[how to do it]

Chef's note: For this recipe, visit your local fish monger and give 'em a smile. He or she will be happy to block cut your tombo for you. There's nothing more tender and delicious than a great piece of fresh-cut tombo tuna!

1. Make the pesto: In a blender, combine all the ingredients (except for the oil) on medium speed until well combined. Add the oil in a slow, steady stream to incorporate. Taste and adjust seasoning if necessary.
2. Prepare the fish: Take two slices of prosciutto and lay them together with a quarter-inch overlapping. Put one piece of tombo in the center of the prosciutto and wrap it up. Repeat with the other piece of tombo. Let the fish sit in the refrigerator for a minimum of 20 minutes so it has time for the prosciutto to rest and set up.
3. Make the reduction: Combine the ingredients in a pot, bring to a boil and then lower to a simmer. Reduce until it coats the back of a spoon.
4. Cook the fish: In a medium sauté pan, get the oil hot (near smoking) and sear the tombo on all sides until the prosciutto is a little crispy. Remove the fish from the pan and slice with a sharp knife.
5. To serve: Spoon some of the balsamic reduction and the pesto onto a plate and arrange tombo slices on top. Garnish with microgreens and edible flowers.

culotte steak + fried onions + chimichurri béarnaise

serves 4 friends | as a main

This is our lightened-up version of a classic, steak and béarnaise. We start with a super-heavy butter hollandaise, but we brighten it up with herbs, red wine vinegar, lemon juice, and some heat from the chile flakes. Put this on a perfectly grilled steak with a little char and you'll have it all working! Steak and béarnaise: It's a beautiful thing!

[for the chimichurri béarnaise]

3 eggs
½ tablespoon freshly squeezed lemon juice
1 teaspoon Tabasco sauce
1 pound butter, clarified
1 teaspoon fresh tarragon
1 cup fresh parsley
1 teaspoon fresh oregano
1 clove fresh garlic, minced
1 teaspoon fresh shallot, minced
1 teaspoon red chile flakes
⅛ cup red wine vinegar
Kosher salt and freshly ground black pepper, to taste

[for the fried onions]

1 yellow onion, sliced into thin rounds
¼ cup buttermilk
1 cup all-purpose flour
1 cup cornstarch
2 cups canola oil, for frying
Kosher salt and freshly ground black pepper, to taste

[for the steak]

2 tablespoons canola oil
4 (8-ounce) culotte steaks
1 cup mizuna (or arugula, mustard, or other fresh spicy greens)

[how to do it]

1. Make the béarnaise: Place the eggs, lemon juice, and Tabasco in a blender and process on medium-low speed until well combined. Add the butter in a slow, steady stream until completely incorporated. Add the remaining ingredients, processing on medium-low speed, until well combined and the mixture is smooth.
2. Make the onions: Soak the sliced onions in the buttermilk for 20 minutes.
3. In a medium bowl, whisk together the flour and cornstarch until well combined.
4. Preheat a deep fryer or oil in a sauté pan to 350°F.
5. Coat the onions with the flour and cornstarch mix. Place the rings in the fryer (or into the pan with hot oil) and cook until golden brown. Remove them from the oil and place on paper towels to drain and stay crispy. Season to taste with salt and pepper.
6. Cook the steaks: In a large sauté pan, heat the oil to very hot (near smoking). Place the steaks in the pan (don't let them touch) and cook until browned on one side, about 5 to 7 minutes. Flip and cook to desired doneness on the second side, about 5 minutes for medium-rare (135°F).
7. To serve: Place each steak in the center of a plate. Top with chimichurri béarnaise, fresh greens, and fried onions. "Killer" Butter Potatoes are awesome with this!

"When I say 'killer' potatoes, I not only mean 'killer' good, I also mean 'killer' like they'll kill you — literally — if you eat them every night! They're so rich and buttery and delicious, they're definitely a special treat for special nights! Indulge!"

'killer' butter potatoes

serves 4 friends | as a side

4 Yukon Gold potatoes
1 cup heavy cream
1 stick (4 ounces) butter
1 cup cream cheese, at room temperature
Kosher salt and white pepper, to taste

[how to do it]

1. Peel and cut each potato into 4 pieces, cover in a pot with cold water, and bring to a boil.
2. The potatoes are done when you can pierce them easily with a knife. Strain the potatoes and mash them in a large bowl.
3. In a separate small pot, combine the cream and butter and bring to a boil. Remove from the heat. Mix the liquid in with the mashed potatoes and add the cream cheese, mashing until well incorporated. Taste and season with salt and pepper.

"A culotte steak is cut from the top cap of the sirloin. It has great flavor and is a great bang for the buck! They love it in Paris!"

corn + chorizo + jalapeño crema

serves 4 friends | as an app or side

Being that we're all about American classics redefined, we wanted this dish to be a nod to good ol' Texas tradition. The recipe was actually developed by a couple of our line cooks at Searsucker and it's turned into one of our bestsellers. People freakin' love it! So, here it is — one of our best-kept secrets out for all of you to make at home!

[for the corn crema]
4 corn cobs, kernels removed and reserved
4 cups water
1 cup buttermilk
1 cup heavy cream
1 guajillo chile, seeded
1 lime, zested and juiced
½ cup sour cream
1 tablespoon granulated sugar
Kosher salt, to taste

[for the sautéed corn]
1 tablespoon canola oil
4 ears corn, kernels removed (throw these cobs into the corn stock for the corn crema too!)
½ cup chorizo, chopped (I like Bilbao)
¼ large red onion, chopped
1 tablespoon fresh cilantro, chopped
1 jalapeño chile, seeded and chopped
Kosher salt and freshly ground black pepper, to taste

[how to do it]

Chef's note: This makes more crema than you'll need for one recipe, but it will keep, refrigerated, for up to 10 days. You can use it in anything that calls for buttermilk or cream with a kick!

1. Make the corn crema: In a large stockpot, bring the cobs and water to a boil and reduce by half (until you have about 2 cups of liquid) and strain. Add the corn stock back to the pot on medium-high heat and add all the remaining ingredients. Bring the liquid to a simmer and cook for 5 minutes. Strain and reserve.
2. Make the sautéed corn: In a medium sauté pan, heat the oil to hot and sauté the corn kernels with the chorizo, onion, cilantro, and jalapeño until the sugars in the corn start to caramelize.
3. Add ½ cup of the crema to the corn in the sauté pan and cook for 1 minute. Place in a bowl and serve immediately.

searsucker's cali belgique short rib sandwich + horseradish sauce

serves 4 to 6 friends | as a main

When we make this recipe, we use about a gallon of Stone Cali Belgique in stock for the braise. Now that's cooking with beer! Of course, when you're preparing this at home, you'll only need 24 ounces to get that great beer kick in the sauce. The trick, when using a beer with this much hops, is to not let it boil, which brings out the bitterness. That's why a low and slow braise at 300°F is the perfect way to go.

[for the short ribs]
2 tablespoons canola or vegetable oil
2 pounds boneless short ribs
4 ribs celery, diced small
2 yellow onions, diced small
3 carrots, diced small
4 cloves fresh garlic, crushed
24 ounces Stone Cali Belgique (or other great Belgian-inspired strong ale)
2 cups beef stock
2 cups chicken stock
2 sprigs fresh thyme
1 tablespoon black peppercorns
2 bay leaves

[for the horseradish sauce]
1 cup sour cream
1 tablespoon Worcestershire sauce
1 tablespoon extra hot horseradish, or more to taste (I love Atomic)
Kosher salt and freshly ground black pepper, to taste

[for the fried onions]
1 yellow onion, sliced into thin rounds
¼ cup buttermilk
1 cup all-purpose flour
1 cup cornstarch
2 cups canola oil, for frying
Kosher salt and freshly ground black pepper, to taste

[finishing touches]
French rolls or the softest roll you can find
Pesto (See recipe, page 33)
Big handful fresh arugula

[how to do it]

1. Preheat oven to 300°F.

2. **Prepare the short ribs:** In a medium sauté pan, heat the oil to near smoking and sear the short ribs on both sides until golden brown. Remove from pan and set aside. In the same pan, sauté the celery, onion, carrots, and garlic until caramelized, about 10 minutes. Place the short rib and vegetable mix into an oven-proof roasting pan and cover with the beer, beef stock, and chicken stock. Add the thyme, peppercorns, and bay leaves, cover with foil, and cook oven for 3½ hours, or until fork tender. Remove from the oven and let cool in the braising liquid. (Once cool, you can portion out the meat, or you can strain the braising liquid and refrigerate the short ribs overnight in the liquid, which will enhance the final flavor. You can reheat the meat with some of the braising liquid in a hot sauté pan before serving.)

3. **Make the horseradish sauce:** In a small bowl, mix all the ingredients together and refrigerate until needed.

4. **Make the onions:** Soak the sliced onions in buttermilk for 20 minutes. In a medium bowl, whisk together the flour and cornstarch until well combined. Preheat a deep fryer or oil in a sauté pan to 350°F. Coat the onions with the flour and cornstarch mix. Place the rings in the fryer or into the pan with hot oil and cook until golden brown. Remove them from the oil and place on paper towels to drain and stay crispy.

5. **Assemble the sandwiches:** At Searsucker we make short rib sandwiches for lunch and here's how we "roll": Take your French roll and fill it with shredded short ribs, dividing the meat equally among the sandwiches. Top with crispy fried onions, 1 tablespoon of horseradish sauce, fresh arugula, and pesto, if desired.

"Pair this sandwich with Stone's Cali Belgique, for sure.
There's a lot of yeasty, malty flavor
in Cali, but also a good amount of hop,
which pairs so, so well with the
fattiness of the short rib."
—Chef Shane

whiskey-braised pork + grilled peaches + baconnaise

serves 4 friends | as a main

Early in my career, horse racing was a big part of my life. I still love it. And I like to have a few things on the menu that remind me of the down-and-dirty excitement and adrenaline of the Derby and the other great classic American races around the country. Grilled peaches, my special mayo made with bacon fat, and a little whiskey thrown in for good measure — that's a horse of a different (and delicious) color!

[for the pork]
2 tablespoons canola oil
2½ pounds pork butt (shoulder), cut into ½-pound pieces
1 carrot, diced large
2 celery stalks, diced large
1 red onion, diced large
1 cup whiskey or bourbon
4 cups chicken stock
¼ cup fresh garlic, chopped large
1 bunch fresh parsley, roughly chopped
1 tablespoon fresh thyme
3 slices bacon, chopped
4 ripe peaches, grilled and quartered
2 tablespoons shallots, minced

[for the "quick" baconnaise]
¼ cup bacon fat, warm
½ cup mayonnaise
Kosher salt and freshly ground black pepper, to taste

[finishing touch]
1 handful fresh parsley, pan fried crispy in canola oil

[how to do it]

Chef's note: This recipe uses a "quick" baconnaise. You can also do the from-scratch version. *See recipe, page 101.*

1. Preheat oven to 250°F.
2. Prepare the pork: In a large roasting pan on top of the stove, heat the oil to near smoking and sear the pork on all sides, about 1 to 2 minutes on each side.
3. Add the carrot, celery, and onion and cook until you get some great caramelization. Deglaze the pan with the whiskey or bourbon and add the chicken stock, garlic, herbs, and enough water to just barely cover the pork pieces.
4. Bring to a boil and place in the oven to braise for 2 to 3 hours, or until the pork is SUPER soft, fork tender, and just ready to give it all up.
5. In a small pan, cook the bacon until crispy, strain from the fat, and toss the warm pieces with the peaches and a little whiskey or bourbon. Set aside. Save the warm bacon fat for the baconnaise.
6. Remove the pork from the braising liquid and keep warm. Strain the liquid into a medium saucepot, add the shallot, and reduce by half.
7. Make the baconnaise: Whisk the warm bacon fat, a little at a time, into the mayonnaise. Season with salt and pepper to taste.
8. To serve: Place a nice dollop of baconnaise on each plate. Warm the meat in the reduced braising liquid and place alongside the baconnaise. Spoon some sauce over each piece of meat, add some grilled peaches, and top with some fried parsley. The FEAST is on! Get dirty with your pork butt!!!

chicken brie sandwich + tarragon aioli

serves 4 friends | as a main

In my opinion, you must have at least one great chicken sandwich on a menu — that's just a given. We do this sandwich with our own fresh tarragon aioli, which — along with the oven-dried tomatoes — gives the brie and the chicken an awesome pop. Put it all between the freshest, crustiest, most delicious bread you can find, and you have one of the greatest lunches, dinners, or midnight snacks known to man!

[for the tomatoes]
8 Roma tomatoes, halved

[for the tarragon aioli]
1 cup mayonnaise
2 tablespoons fresh tarragon, minced
1 tablespoon freshly squeezed lemon juice
Kosher salt and freshly ground black pepper, to taste

[for the sandwiches]
4 (6-ounce) chicken breasts, boneless and skinless
4 ounces Brie cheese
4 ciabatta rolls
2 cups watercress
Whole grain mustard (or your favorite)

[how to do it]

Chef's note: You want to do the oven-dried tomatoes the night before you make these sandwiches, or just have them on hand. They're great for pastas, and a whole bunch of other things!

1. Preheat oven to 250°F.
2. **Make the oven-dried tomatoes:** Place them on a roasting pan in the oven for a minimum of 6 hours or overnight. This will allow them to concentrate their flavor as well as bring out their natural sugars.
3. **Make the aioli:** In a blender on medium speed, combine all the ingredients until smooth. Taste what you've got and see if it needs salt or pepper.
4. Preheat a grill to medium or oven to 350°F.
5. **Cook the chicken:** Grill the breasts for approximately 5 minutes on each side, until the meat is just firm.
6. **Now for the final step:** Place the grilled meat in an ovenproof dish and lay tomatoes and brie on top. Bake in the oven until the cheese is nice and melted. Serve on the ciabatta roll with watercress, mustard, and tarragon aioli. This one is great with a cold red or brown ale or a cool glass of chardonnay.

stuffed chicken + sourdough stuffing + whiskey gravy

serves 4 friends | as a main

This recipe is our take on a classic French roulade (meat rolled around something incredibly delicious, like our chicken chorizo). We've combined it with an American comfort-food classic: roasted chicken with stuffing and gravy. It's a feel-good feast for the whole family!

[for the chicken chorizo]
2 pounds chicken thigh meat, ground
4 tablespoons fresh garlic, minced
2 tablespoons paprika
2 teaspoons onion powder
2 teaspoons ground cumin
2 tablespoons kosher salt
1 tablespoon freshly ground black pepper

[for the chicken]
1 whole chicken, deboned and split in half
2 sticks (8 ounces) butter, cut into cubes, divided use
6 sprigs fresh thyme, divided use

[for the stuffing]
10 cups sourdough bread, cubed
½ stick (2 ounces) butter
¼ cup onions, diced
¼ cup celery, diced
¼ cup leeks, diced
⅛ cup white wine
3 cups heavy cream
2 egg yolks
1 cup freshly shredded Parmesan cheese
3 sprigs fresh thyme

[for the corn broth]
6 cups water
6 corn cobs, smoked, if desired

[for the gravy]
½ cup whiskey, flambéed
1 lemon, juiced
¼ cup heavy cream
2 tablespoons cornstarch
Kosher salt and freshly ground black pepper, to taste

[how to do it]

1. Make the chorizo: In a large bowl, combine all the ingredients well.
2. Make the chicken: Stuff each half chicken with 1 cup of the chorizo mixture. Roll tightly, tie with butcher's twine, and place in a heavy-duty plastic bag. Add 1 stick of butter and 3 sprigs of thyme to each bag. Vacuum seal, or seal as tightly as possible. Bring a pot of water or a water bath to 155°F and add the chicken, still in the bags. Cook for 1 hour and transfer to an ice bath immediately.
3. Make the stuffing: Preheat broiler. Arrange the bread cubes evenly on a sheet tray and toast until light brown, turning occasionally. Remove and allow to cool. Reduce oven to 325°F.
4. In a large sauté pan on medium-high heat, melt the butter and add the onions, celery, and leeks. Sweat the vegetables until they become translucent. Add the wine and reduce until most of the liquid is gone.
5. In a medium bowl, whisk together the cream and yolks. Add the Parmesan and thyme, and mix to combine well.
6. Add the cream and vegetable mixture to the remaining chorizo mixture in the large bowl. Mix well. Pour into two large parchment-lined pans or sheet trays, cover with foil or another sheet tray, and press for 30 minutes. Remove the foil or sheet tray and bake for 30 minutes uncovered, or until the stuffing is set and nice and brown on top.
7. Make the corn broth: In a large pot, bring the water and corn cobs to a boil and reduce the broth by two-thirds until you have about 4 cups. Strain. Add the corn stock back to the pot on medium-high heat.
8. Make the gravy: To the corn broth, add the whiskey and lemon juice. In a small bowl, take 1 cup of the broth and whisk in the cream and cornstarch until smooth. Whisk the cream mixture into the pot, allow it to almost come to a simmer, and stir well. Taste, adjust seasoning, and strain.
9. To serve: Slice the chicken into generous rounds and serve with a square of stuffing and drizzle of gravy.

brussels sprouts + candied walnuts + anchovy vinaigrette

serves 4 friends | as a side

I asked all my chefs at my restaurants to each do their own version of brussels sprouts. I love them, and they're one of the most misunderstood veggies out there. Once people have our brussels, their faces light up. "Oh my God!" they say, mouths full and chins dripping with sauce, "I hate brussels sprouts, but I LOVE these!" Brussels with muscles — that's how we do veg!

[for the candied walnuts]
2 egg whites
2 cups shelled walnuts
1 cup granulated sugar

[for the vinaigrette]
4 cloves fresh garlic
5 white anchovies
1 serrano chile, seeded
1 tablespoon honey
1 cup red wine
1 cup olive oil

[for the brussels sprouts]
Canola oil, for frying
2 pounds fresh brussels sprouts

[how to do it]

1. Preheat oven to 350°F.
2. **Make the candied walnuts:** In a medium bowl or mixer, whip the egg whites until frothy, about 1 to 2 minutes on medium speed. Stir in the the walnuts by hand and coat well. Put the sugar in a medium bowl. Take the walnuts out of the egg whites and toss them with the sugar. Spread the nuts on a sheet tray and toast in the oven until golden brown, about 12 to 15 minutes. Allow to cool before using.
3. **Make the vinaigrette:** In blender on medium-low speed, process all the ingredients (except the oil) until well combined. Add the oil in a slow, steady stream until fully incorporated.
4. Preheat a deep fryer to 350°F or heat oil in a large sauté pan to very hot (near smoking).
5. **Cook the brussels sprouts:** Fry the sprouts until the leaves begin to brown. Pull them out of the oil and drain on paper towels.
6. **To serve:** Place the sprouts in a large serving bowl and toss with the anchovy vinaigrette and candied walnuts. Taste and adjust seasoning if necessary. Serve immediately.

RESERVED FOR
DINNER
urlap

★ WEST EATS MEAT ★

BURLAP

MY BUSINESS PARTNER JAMES LIKES TO KEEP THE PEDAL TO THE METAL — he keeps us going as fast and as hard as we possibly can (which is great). So, not more than a year or so after we opened Searsucker, he came to me and said he had a great location in Del Mar Highlands Town Center (yes, he wanted to go for the mall experience!). I told him I thought he was crazy — the space he was talking about had previously been a video store — and I said "no way" and "I don't think we can possibly do it." I did say that only our interior designer, Thomas Schoos (who designed Searsucker), could possibly talk me into it. So Thomas came down from L.A., snapped his fingers a couple of times and said, "Dahling, I will make the space incredible!" He asked me what kind of cuisine we wanted to do here. I told him I wanted it to be an "unapologetic white boy doing Asian food," so that's how Burlap's identity, "Asian Cowboy Cuisine," was born. Thomas did a phenomenal job on this one — over the top. We've got koi ponds, fire pits, and giant Chinese dragon masks along with Texas longhorns, old explorer gear, and an incredible carved-wood bar that just knocks your boots off when you first see it! We developed a menu using classic Asian ingredients — garlic, scallions, lemongrass, soy, wasabi, ginger — and putting our American twist on Asian classics and having fun with it. We're fond of saying: "Asian Cowboy: Where the West Eats Meat." We decided on the name Burlap after going down our list of fabric options (we decided right away that Silk was not going to work) and realizing that burlap — while it's not beautiful or sexy — is a tough, durable fabric that you would use to carry your spices, rices, teas, and coffees as you travel around the world. And the more you travel, the more ports of entry you go to, the more tattered it gets, and the more personality it has. And that's what we wanted Burlap to be: fun, comfortable, well-worn, worldly, and adventurous all in one.

Chef Anthony Sinsay

When the time came to find someone to head up the kitchen long-term at Burlap, I decided that our restaurant expansions would be a great opportunity to work with chefs around San Diego that I really admired and had done events with. One of those guys was Anthony Sinsay. I absolutely love the guy. He brings so much flair, so much style to his cooking, and he's worked in some of the best kitchens in town. His pedigree is impeccable, he's young, he's passionate, and I was fortunate to be able to bring him in to Burlap, to show him what I had done with the Asian Cowboy concept, and then to let him run with it. He gave me his own Filipino interpretations and takes on the food, in addition to developing a whole bunch of awesome new dishes. Anthony has done great things for Burlap, and I just love working with him. We're two wasabi peas in a pod (as much as a "tong chef"and a "tweezer chef" can be!).

house-made kimchee

serves 8 to 10 friends | as an app or side

I said it before, and I'll say it again: I'm a sucker for pickled whatever! Anthony is a kimchee master (black belt, I think!) and it would be a crime to have him at a restaurant without offering this on the menu. Like most good things, this one takes a little patience, but it's so worth waiting for. My advice: Share this with your date or loved one. The garlic and chile paste are not for the faint of heart, and it's better to share it than to go it alone!

¼ cup kosher salt
1 tablespoon granulated sugar
1 gallon water
1 head Napa cabbage, cut into 10 pieces lengthwise, keeping the core intact
1 tablespoon fresh garlic, chopped
1 tablespoon fresh ginger, chopped
2 tablespoons fish sauce
1 tablespoon plus 1½ teaspoons honey
1 bunch scallions, cut in half lengthwise
3 tablespoons Korean chile paste
1 cup daikon radish, grated
8 oysters, live, freshly shucked
8 (16-ounce) mason jars, sterilized

[how to do it]

1. In a large container, dissolve the salt and sugar in water and submerge the cabbage. Let the cabbage brine in the solution for 2 hours. Drain completely and let it dry for 1 hour.
2. In a large bowl, combine the cabbage with all the remaining ingredients, thoroughly coating all the pieces and rubbing the mix into each leaf of cabbage.
3. Equally divide the rubbed cabbage and remaining liquid among the mason jars (make sure you have 1 oyster in each), and seal tightly.
4. Refrigerate for a minimum of 1 week and up to 2 months. Serve with grilled meats, fish, or anything else you want. I put that stuff on everything!

tuna poke + shishito aioli + guacamole + pepper crab

serves 4 friends | as an app

Poke is one of those things. If you have an Asian restaurant, you gotta have poke. But traditional poke is really just fresh fish with a little bit of soy. Being that we don't like to do anything unless it's sensational, we created this rather extravagant poke dish with albacore and crab meat, accompanied by a luscious, spicy aioli and a chunky guacamole (SoCal, baby!).

[for the shishito pepper aioli]

1 cup shishito peppers, stemmed (available at Asian markets)
2 tablespoons freshly squeezed lemon juice, divided use
1 tablespoon tamari or regular soy sauce
2 egg yolks
1 clove fresh garlic
1 tablespoon Dijon mustard
1 cup olive oil blend (80 canola/20 olive oil)
Kosher salt, to taste

[for the tuna mixture]

1 cup fresh tombo albacore tuna, diced small
2 tablespoons tamari soy sauce
½ jalapeño chile, charred over flame, stemmed and minced (leave all the seeds, some seeds, or no seeds, depending on how hot you like it)
1 scallion, charred over flame
1 teaspoon Sriracha chile sauce

[for the guacamole]

1 ripe avocado
¼ cup red onion, diced small
1 tablespoon freshly squeezed lemon juice
Kosher salt, to taste

[for the pepper crab]

½ pound (or 8-ounce can) jumbo lump crabmeat
½ teaspoon nanami togarashi (Japanese mixed chile pepper spice powder; available at Asian markets)

[for the yuzu vinaigrette/pea shoot salad]

1 tablespoon yuzu juice (available at Asian markets, or you can sub lime juice)
3 tablespoons olive oil
1 cup pea shoots
Kosher salt and freshly ground black pepper, to taste

[finishing touch]

Taro or sweet potato chips

[how to do it]

Chef's note: This recipe makes more aioli than you'll need. Store the leftover aioli in the fridge for up to 2 weeks.

1. Preheat oven to 400°F.
2. Make the aioli: In a small ovenproof dish, combine the shishito peppers, 1 tablespoon lemon juice, and tamari and roast in the oven until toasted and blistered. Allow to cool completely. In a blender combine the egg yolks, remaining lemon juice, garlic, and Dijon mustard and process until it becomes pale yellow. Add the shishito peppers and blend on high while drizzling in the oil in a slow, steady stream. Season to taste with salt. Set aside.
3. Assemble the tuna mixture: In a bowl toss together all the ingredients and set aside.
4. Make the guacamole: In a bowl combine all ingredients by lightly mashing with the avocado. Taste and adjust seasoning, if necessary. (Be sure to keep the guacamole pit in the mixture so it keeps its bright green color.)
5. Make the pepper crab: In a medium bowl mix the crab with the nanami togarashi. Add ½ cup of the shishito aioli and toss well to coat. Set aside.
6. Make the vinaigrette: Whisk together the yuzu and the olive oil to combine well. Mix in pea shoots and season to taste with salt and pepper.
7. To assemble: In a cocktail glass, first place the pepper crab/shishito aioli mixture, then a layer of guacamole. Finish with the tuna mixture and garnish with the yuzu vinaigrette/pea shoot salad. Serve with taro chips.

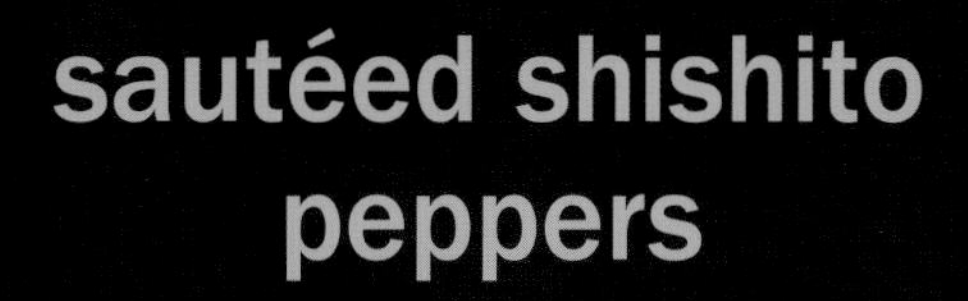

sautéed shishito peppers

These sweet-and-spicy little babies are one of the best-selling apps we have at Burlap, and they're so good you hardly have to do anything to them! This preparation will work for any amount of peppers, so go out and get as many as you can find!

[how to do it]

1. In a medium sauté pan, heat 1 to 2 tablespoons of canola oil to very hot.
2. Add the peppers and cook until they begin to shrivel (about 3 minutes). Add ponzu sauce to taste and toss in the pan to coat. Transfer to a serving dish and devour!

"Shishito peppers are a traditional Japanese pepper, and the interesting thing about them is that only about one in every ten is actually hot. The word 'shishito' actually means 'lucky' because the person who gets one of the hot peppers is considered to be lucky."

— Chef Anthony

miso soup + sautéed mushrooms + scallions

serves 4 friends | as an app

Nothing warms your soul better before a meal than a great bowl of miso soup. Chef Anthony's take on miso includes some meatiness from sautéed mushrooms and some chewiness from wakame, which is a Korean seaweed. If you're at an Asian market and you see some other ingredients you like, get 'em and throw 'em in. With this miso as your base, you can't go wrong!

4 cups water
1 (2-inch piece) kombu (Japanese seaweed; available at most Asian markets)
2 cups bonito flakes (available at most Asian markets)
9 ounces white miso paste
½ cup tofu, diced into ½-inch cubes
¼ cup wakame (Korean dried seaweed; available at most Asian markets)
¼ cup gently sautéed sliced mushrooms (I like oysters or enokis)
¼ cup scallions, julienned

[how to do it]

1. In a stockpot bring the water and kombu to a hard simmer. Remove the kombu, add the bonito flakes, and allow to steep for 1 hour.
2. Press the liquid through a strainer lined with a coffee filter into a clean saucepot. Bring the liquid to a simmer and whisk in the miso paste.
3. **To serve:** Place the tofu, wakame, mushrooms, and scallions in bowls. Pour the soup into bowls from the side.

asian clam chowder

serves 4 friends | as an app

Here's another great example of what happens when Asia meets a classic American dish like clam chowder. You've got the familiar butter, cream, celery, and onions, but we've also kicked it with additions of Chinese sausage, taro root, bonito flakes, and dashi, a basic Asian fish broth. The result is a creamy chowder with deep, rich flavors from the sea. This is my go-to heart-warmer on a damp, cold, drizzly day!

[for the dashi]

4 cups water
1 (2-inch piece) kombu (type of seaweed; available at Asian markets)
4 cups bonito flakes (available at Asian markets and grocery stores)

[for the chowder]

4 tablespoons butter
2 cups celery, diced
2 cups Spanish onion, diced
4 cloves fresh garlic, chopped
2 teaspoons fresh thyme, chopped
1½ cups Chinese sausage (similar to dried, cured salami; available at Asian markets and some supermarkets)
4 cups taro root, diced (or you can sub sweet potato or yam)
2 cups heavy cream
2 pounds fresh Manila clams
Kosher salt and freshly ground black pepper, to taste

[finishing touch]

Crusty bread slices

[how to do it]

1. **Make the dashi:** In a saucepan, bring the kombu and water to a boil and turn it off. Remove the kombu, add the bonito flakes, and steep for 1 hour. Strain through a cheesecloth.
2. **Make the chowder:** In a large saucepan, heat the butter on medium-high and cook the celery, onions, and garlic until translucent. Add the thyme and cook for 1 more minute.
3. Add the Chinese sausage and taro root, cover with dashi, and simmer until the taro is cooked and has thickened the broth, about 20 to 30 minutes.
4. Add the cream and the clams and cook covered until all the clams open. Discard any clams that do not open after 10 to 12 minutes. Adjust seasoning with salt and pepper, if necessary.
5. Serve with your favorite crusty bread — you'll need it to soak up the amazing sauce!

"What's cool about using taro root in this recipe is that you don't need the traditional addition of a roux (butter and flour). The taro has such a high starch content that it thickens the chowder all by itself."
— Chef Anthony

mussels adobo

serves 4 friends | as a main

When it comes to Filipino-style cooking, Chef Anthony is the man! Adobo is the national dish of the Philippines, and this preparation has caught on fire at Burlap (not literally!). It's quickly becoming one of our most-popular all-time dishes. Traditionally, adobo is done with chicken and pork, but here we use it as the liquid to steam our mussels, so it's literally an "East meets West" kind of idea — the mussels being a traditionally French type of dish, and the adobo being Asian. By the time you're sopping up the last drops of sauce with your crusty bread, you should have adobo dripping down your chin!

[for the mussels]
4 tablespoons canola oil
½ cup Spanish onion, sliced
4 cloves fresh garlic, sliced
1 jalapeño chile, sliced
2 pounds fresh black mussels, debearded and rinsed
4 tablespoons soy sauce
4 tablespoons distilled white vinegar
½ cup water
4 tablespoons canned coconut milk
2 tablespoons butter, cold

[finishing touch]
Crusty bread slices

[how to do it]

1. In a large sauté pan, heat the oil to hot and sauté the onions, garlic, and jalapeño until they soften and become aromatic.
2. Add the mussels and toss to coat them.
3. Add the soy sauce, vinegar, and water. Cover with a lid and steam until all the mussels have opened. Remove the mussels to a bowl and cover to keep warm. Discard any mussels that have not opened after 10 to 12 minutes.
4. Reduce the cooking liquid by half. Add the coconut milk and reduce again, until the mixture thickens. Swirl in the butter, and add the mussels back to the sauce.
5. Serve with plenty of your favorite toasted bread.

crispy skinned salmon + green papaya salad + coconut lobster sauce

serves 4 friends | as a main

Chef Anthony is a master at combining Asian influences from all over the world into one really cool dish AND he's a good-looking man to boot! Here, he's managed to combine traditional Thai elements in the sauce with traditional Vietnamese elements in the green papaya slaw. The sauce for this dish is off the hook! It's basically a lobster bisque made with coconut milk. The slaw adds a clean, refreshing element and ties the whole plate together, making it light but also very hearty and satisfying.

[for the papaya salad]

1 cup green papaya, julienned (available at Asian produce markets)
½ cup carrot, julienned
½ cup jicama, julienned

[for the dressing]

½ teaspoon fresh ginger, grated
3 cloves fresh garlic, grated
2 tablespoons fish sauce
2 tablespoons freshly squeezed lime juice
2 tablespoons granulated sugar
2 tablespoons light brown sugar
1 Thai chile, seeded and minced
¼ cup mint, sliced into thin strips

[for the coconut lobster sauce]

¼ cup canola oil
1 stalk lemongrass, chopped
3 cloves fresh garlic, chopped
2 teaspoons fresh ginger, chopped
2 Thai chiles, split in half
2 Roma tomatoes, diced large
1 lobster body and shells, cleaned of tail and claw meat
¼ cup light brown sugar
2 kaffir lime leaves
2 tablespoons tomato paste
½ cup Xiao Tsing wine (Mirin also works; available at Asian markets)
1 teaspoon fish sauce
2 tablespoons freshly squeezed lime juice
3 cups canned coconut milk

[for the fish]

2 to 3 tablespoons canola oil, or as needed
4 (6-ounce) salmon filets, skin on
Kosher salt and freshly ground black pepper, to taste
4 tablespoons butter
2 to 3 cloves fresh garlic, minced
Fresh mixed herbs, minced (I like lemongrass, cilantro, and thyme)

[how to do it]

Chef's note: This Coconut Lobster Sauce recipe uses the empty shells and body of a boiled lobster. This is a great way to utilize the leftover parts of a lobster whenever you've cooked a bunch up. Make this sauce (or just a plain lobster stock) whenever you've cooked your own lobsters. It's a great thing to have handy in the freezer!

1. Make the salad: Toss the papaya, carrot, and jicama together in a bowl and set aside.
2. Make the dressing: In a medium bowl, whisk together all the ingredients and set aside.
3. Make the sauce: In a large saucepan, heat the oil to medium high and sauté the lemongrass, garlic, ginger, Thai chiles, and tomatoes until the tomatoes start to thicken. Add the lobster body and shells, brown sugar, lime leaves, and tomato paste. Cook, stirring, for about 2 minutes. Deglaze the bottom of the pan with the wine, fish sauce, and lime juice, scraping up and dissolving any solids from the bottom, and reduce slightly. Add the coconut milk and simmer for 1 hour.
4. Prepare the fish: In a large sauté pan, heat the oil slightly. Season the flesh side of the salmon with salt and

pepper. On the skin side, open the salmon scales by running your hands over the skin of the fish against the grain.
5. Place the fish in the sauté pan, skin side down, and sear evenly by pressing the fish gently into the pan. Cook until the skin starts to crisp and brown. Flip the fish over and add butter, garlic, and herbs. Baste the fish with the butter to finish crisping the skin over high heat.
6. When the salmon skin begins to crackle, remove the pieces from the pan and put them on plates.
7. To serve: Re-whisk the salad dressing to combine well, and dress the papaya salad. Strain the lobster sauce, spoon some onto each plate, top with the salmon, and finish with the slaw.

skin-on searing 101

Here's Chef Anthony's step-by-step guide to searing and plating a skin-on piece of fish.

[1] Start with the freshest piece of salmon.

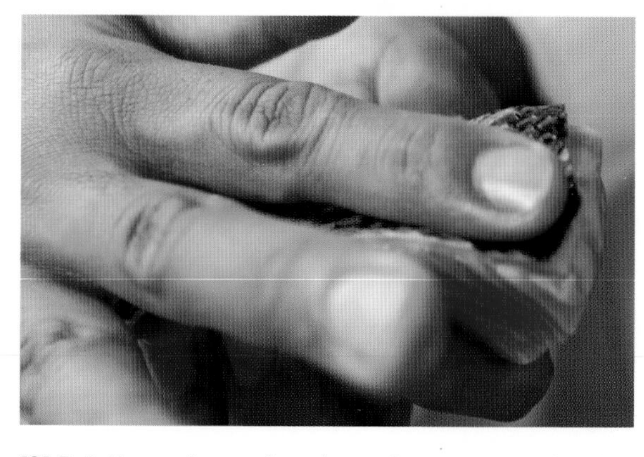

[2] Rub the scales against the grain to open up the skin.

[3] Season with salt and pepper.

[4] Put the fish in a very hot sauté pan, skin side down. Apply some pressure with your hand or a spatula, but do not move it.

[5] Flip the fish when you see the skin is crisping.

[6] Baste the fish with the buttery liquid.

[7] Sauce the plate.

[8] Top the sauce with the fish.

[10] Behold the finished dish!

[9] Arrange the topping and garnish.

garlic noodles + mushrooms

serves 4 friends | as a side

We love this as a side dish or a main course (perfect for veggies or vegans). This is our combination of the traditional Asian chow mein with the addition of local produce that we like to use to highlight the tons of great farms we have close by. The recipe lists traditional Asian mushroom varieties, but you can play around with using any you like. Same goes with the veggies: Anthony is fond of throwing in a bunch of fresh broccoli. Go to your local farmers market, see what's fresh, and let that be your inspiration for this dish!

[for the garlic purée]
1 cup whole fresh garlic cloves, peeled
Water, to cover

[for the noodles]
½ cup canola oil
¾ cup shiitake mushrooms, sliced
¾ cup cremini mushrooms, sliced
¾ cup honshimeji mushrooms, sliced
½ cup oyster sauce
3 cups chow mein noodles, cooked
3 tablespoons butter (or soy spread for vegans)

[finishing touches]
Fresh scallions, chopped
Fresh raw or steamed vegetables (almost anything: broccoli, carrots, cabbage…), if desired

[how to do it]

1. Make the garlic purée: In a small saucepot, boil the garlic cloves in water until soft and fork tender. Place them in a blender with the remaining water from the pot and process on high until smooth.
2. Make the noodles: In a large sauté pan heat the canola oil on high until it is just starts to smoke. Add the mushrooms and sauté until they are caramelized, browned, and crispy.
3. Stir in the oyster sauce and 4 tablespoons of the garlic purée. Add the noodles and toss gently with the butter, being sure to coat each noodle with sauce.
4. To serve: Garnish the mushrooms and noodles with scallions and veggies, if desired, and serve immediately with plenty of chilled glasses and some cold beer!

drunken duck sandwich

serves 4 friends | as a main

All right, I admit it! This is my favorite sandwich at Burlap and — no — it's not just because the duck is drunk! This sandwich is an awesome blend of the traditional elements you find in a chicken salad mixed with the traditional Asian element of duck. The fruit and nuts mixed in give this great crunch — and when I dive into one of these, there's an explosion of tangy, moist duck in my mouth — and on my shirt, pants, and shoes. I love it! I've got duck coming out all over!

[for the drunken duck]

1½ cups cooked chicken, diced (mix of white and dark meat)
1½ cups cooked duck legs, skinned, deboned, and diced
¾ cup celery, diced
¾ cup red onion, diced
¾ cup dried cherries (rehydrated in ½ cup red wine and ½ cup bourbon and drained)
¾ cup macadamia nuts, toasted and roughly chopped
¾ cup mayonnaise
⅔ cup Dijon mustard
Kosher salt and freshly ground black pepper, to taste

[finishing touches]

4 hoagie rolls
Tomato slices
Butter lettuce leaves

[how to do it]

1. Preheat oven to 350°F
2. **Make the drunken duck:** In a medium bowl, combine all the ingredients and adjust the seasoning to taste.
3. Toast the hoagie rolls slightly.
4. **To serve:** Lay tomato slices and lettuce inside each roll and fill each roll with the drunken duck mixture.

grilled new york sirloin + ginger butter

serves 4 friends | as a main

What's better than a great piece of steak, grilled perfectly? Nothing! For really great cuts of meat, most of what you want to do is get out of the way and let the meat do the talking! So, for this, get your grill nice and hot, sear it up, get some great grill marks and caramelization on the crust, and pull it off at medium-rare (135°F). Then you let a nice fat hunk of ginger butter melt on top, as you cut into it and take your first mouth-blasting bite … and wash it down with a great California Cab or red Bordeaux!

[for the ginger butter]
2 sticks (8 ounces) butter, softened
1 tablespoon fresh ginger, grated
1 tablespoon fresh garlic, chopped
1 tablespoon scallions, chopped
Kosher salt, to taste

[for the steaks]
4 (10-ounce) New York sirloin steaks, trimmed and cap removed (you can get your butcher to do this)
Kosher salt and freshly ground black pepper, to taste
1 stick (4 ounces) butter, melted
Fresh herbs for the melted butter, if desired

[finishing touches]
Charred scallion
Micro cilantro
Hajikami (Japanese pickled ginger root; available at Asian markets)

[how to do it]

1. Make the ginger butter: In a mixer, combine all the ingredients and turn it out on a sheet of parchment paper and form it into a log or cylinder. Roll the parchment tightly around the butter, making sure to not overlap the paper into the butter roll. Refrigerate for a minimum of 2 hours. Butter should be solid before use.
2. Preheat a grill or a grill pan on a gas range on medium-high heat.
3. Prepare the steaks: Season the steaks liberally with salt and pepper to taste.
4. When ready to cook, place the steaks on the grill grates at a 45-degree angle (this will give you those beautiful cross-hatch grill marks) and allow them to sear for approximately 3 minutes (do not move or lift them off the grill). Brush the steaks periodically with the melted butter.
5. Check steaks by gently lifting a corner to see if they will naturally release. They are ready to turn when they release easily from the grill. Turn each steak to the opposite 45-degree angle on the same side and cook for another 1 to 2 minutes. Flip steaks over and repeat the searing at both 45-degree angles until they are cooked to the desired doneness (medium rare is an internal temperature of 135°F).
6. To serve: Plate each steak with your favorite side dishes, top the steaks with a thick pad of ginger butter, and garnish with scallion, micro cilantro, and Hajikami. Then take a deep breath as that ginger butter melts and you smell nothing but goodness!

"The secret to a great grilled steak? Put it on the grill and don't finagle it. Leave it be, and let the food be food. When it's ready, flip it over, but don't go touching it and messing with it before that."
— Chef Anthony

sweet potato fries + ginger aioli

serves 2 friends | as a side

As if something coming out of the deep fryer isn't going to be delicious enough, we go ahead and toss our sweet potato fries in brown butter, just for that extra bang. Then we pair them with a ginger aioli dipping sauce, so you've got everything working for you. Sweet, salty, buttery, with ginger zing — these babies are finger-suckin' good!

[for the ginger aioli]

1 cup mayonnaise
1 tablespoon tamari or regular soy sauce
2 tablespoons rice wine vinegar
2 teaspoons granulated sugar
3 tablespoons pickled ginger (aka sushi ginger)

[for the fries]

2 sweet potatoes, peeled and cut into ¼-inch fries
2 tablespoons canola oil
1 stick (4 ounces) butter
Peanut or canola oil, for pan frying
Kosher salt, to taste

[how to do it]

1. Make the aioli: In a blender, combine all ingredients on high until smooth. Refrigerate until ready to use.
2. Preheat oven to 350°F.
3. Make the fries: Toss the cut potatoes in the canola oil, and roast in the oven until they are just cooked, about 15 to 20 minutes. Remove the potatoes from the oven and place them in the freezer until they are frozen through, about 30 minutes.
4. In a small saucepan, heat the butter until it starts to brown and becomes nutty in aroma. Set aside.
5. In a large saucepan, heat the frying oil to 365°F (just smoking) and fry the frozen sweet potatoes until crispy. Drain on paper towels, then toss in a bowl with the brown butter and season with salt.
6. Serve with the ginger aioli on the side.

spam fried rice

serves 4 friends | as a main

Nobody I know makes Spam fried rice that can beat Anthony Sinsay's. The guy grew up with it (it's a traditional Filipino comfort food) so you know he can rock it. This is a dish you can eat any time of the day or night. Home late from the party? Whip some up. Breakfast time? Add a few extra eggs. Quick lunch at home? Eat it cold, straight out of the container. It's great any way and any time you got it!

¼ cup canola oil
1 tablespoon sesame oil
1 large carrot, diced small
1 Spanish onion, diced small
½ teaspoon fresh ginger, chopped
3 cloves fresh garlic, finely chopped
1½ cups Spam, diced small
3 cups cooked jasmine rice (preferably day-old)
Kosher salt and freshly ground black pepper, to taste
1 bunch scallions, chopped
1 teaspoon olive oil
1 egg

[how to do it]

1. In a wok or deep sauté pan, heat the canola and sesame oil just until it starts to smoke. Add the carrot, onion, ginger, and garlic and sauté until they start to caramelize and brown slightly.
2. Add the Spam and toss, cooking until it is slightly caramelized.
3. Stir in the rice and mix thoroughly until each grain is coated, being careful to not smash the grains. Season with salt and pepper. (Warning! Do not add soy sauce. Traditional fried rice should be kept clean!)
4. Add the scallions and toss gently until incorporated.
5. When ready to serve the dish: Break the egg into the rice and mix thoroughly to scramble the egg from the warmth of the rice. (This makes for a dramatic flair that will wow your guests.) Serve in bowls.
6. Alternate presentation: Fry an egg in olive oil for each person and serve atop the rice.

"In my house, growing up, we never wasted anything, so this was a way to utilize leftover rice and any vegetables that needed to be cooked or finished. You can throw almost any kind of vegetable into this and it'll work. I also grew up loving Spam, because we always had that around."

— Chef Anthony

lobster avocado scramble

serves 2 friends | as a main

This is one of our most popular brunch items at Burlap, and it's a great way to use up all the little pieces from a cooked lobster once you've devoured the tail and the claw meat. We cook the eggs slow, adding butter at various stages. They finish nice and creamy, and when served with chunks of lobster and fresh chives, they are fluffy, soft, and sexy! Try making this for your significant other when you want to say "I'm diggin' your scene, baby." And forget the orange juice with this one: Champagne all the way!

[for the poached lobster]
2 gallons water
1 cup white wine
2 lemons, sliced in half, juiced
1 teaspoon cloves
1 shallot, sliced
3 fresh garlic cloves, crushed
2 teaspoons black peppercorns
1 bunch fresh parsley
1 sprig fresh thyme
1 live Maine lobster

[for the eggs]
3 tablespoons butter, divided use
6 eggs, beaten with a whisk
¾ cup lobster meat, cooked and chopped
3 tablespoons fontina cheese, shredded

[finishing touches]
2 tablespoons fresh chives, chopped
Kosher salt, to taste
½ ripe avocado, sliced
Scallions, julienned
Additional lobster claw or tail meat

[how to do it]

Chef's note: I'm including the basic preparation for poaching a lobster here, so you can also use it to make other dishes featuring lobster, like my lobster risotto. (See recipe, page 131.) You can play around with the proportions of this recipe — if you have more lobster meat than the recipe calls for, for example, throw it in! If you like more cheese, throw it in! And you can easily adapt this recipe to feed four, six, or eight people by simply multiplying the ingredients.

1. Poach the lobster: In a large pot, bring the water, white wine, lemon halves, and juice to a rolling a boil.
2. Combine the cloves, shallot, garlic, peppercorns, parsley, and thyme in a cheesecloth, tie with butcher's twine, and put it in the pot as the water heats up. (Some chefs will tell you to tie the bundle to a pot handle so that you can find it later, but it's a huge piece of cheesecloth, so you can't miss it!)
3. Add the lobster and boil for 5 minutes.
4. Remove the lobster and submerge it immediately in an ice bath to stop the cooking. When cool, carefully remove the shell from the lobster and reserve ¾ cup of the meat for this recipe. Save the remaining meat and shells for other recipes. (For Chef Anthony's step-by-step tips on breaking down a lobster, see page 132.)
5. Make the eggs: In a nonstick sauté pan, melt 1 tablespoon of butter over low heat. Add the eggs and cook slowly over moderate low heat. After a couple of minutes, stir in 1 more tablespoon of butter. Once the eggs are cooked halfway, add the lobster meat, fontina cheese, and the final tablespoon of butter. Stir constantly until the eggs are cooked through (they should be soft and silky).
6. To serve: Finish with chopped chives and season with salt to taste. If desired, garnish with avocado slices, scallions, and additional lobster claw or tail meat.

[Chef Anthony's Cooking Tip: The secret to great scrambled eggs? Keep it low and slow — scrambled eggs take more than 2 minutes! Low heat, stir the eggs gently, and once they start to come together, add some butter ... then add more butter at the end. Fat is flavor, but butter is better.]

ging

am

WITH THINGS GOING GANGBUSTERS IN DEL MAR, JAMES AND I SET OUR SIGHTS ON "THE EAST" — La Mesa, California. James took me out there one day and showed me a fabulous space with a big outdoor patio and big garage-door windows that opened to the street. He asked me what I thought I could do here. It occurred to me that this was my chance to realize my dream of doing a barbecue-and-fried-chicken kind of restaurant. We decided that our core concept would be "meat market" with a "rustic American" menu that featured what we came to refer to as "meat overload." We piled on alligator, Andouille, pork, sheep, goat, beef of every size, flavor, and texture — and we just had a ball with it. When it was time to name this restaurant, the choice seemed obvious to all of us. Gingham is the comfortable, light fabric you wear in warm weather — it's classic American and it's what you wear to the endless summer barbecue.

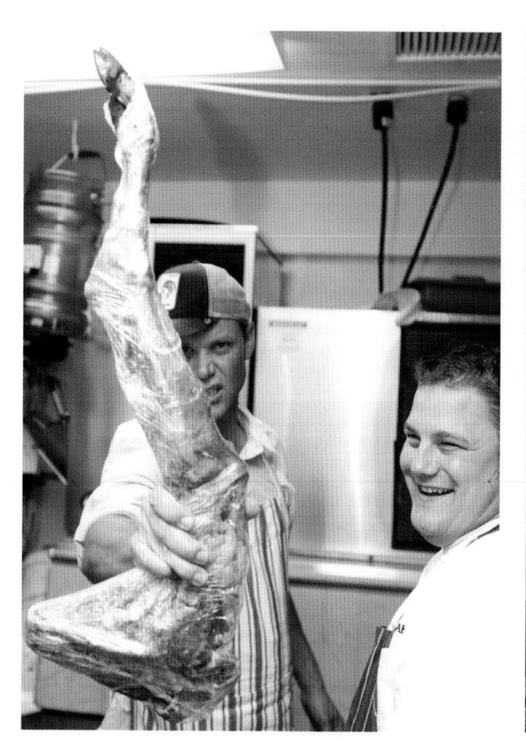

Chef Ryan Studebaker

When I needed barbecue-and-meat experts for my kitchen in La Mesa, I knew Ryan Studebaker and his sous chef Joel Cammet (pictured below, left) were my guys. Joel, who's from Georgia, really "gets" barbecue, and — paired with Ryan and his culinary talents — these two are the "All-American BBQ Dream Team." Ryan has really developed our menu, with a whole bunch of great dishes that incorporate Cajun, Creole, and Southwestern flavors and that highlight the true beauty of the "low and slow" approach to cooking. We like to call Ryan "Big Smoke" because he gets down 'n dirty with the smoker, works it with style, and takes the most classic ideas of barbecue and good ol' Southern-style cooking and makes them fresh, new, and exciting. (Before I hired him, I thought his name was Ryan King, because he had been dating the sweetest girl in the kitchen for a few years...now I know his name is Studebaker — and you know a Malarkey's gotta love a Studebaker!) So, what do I do when I want to find out what's going on "out East" in La Mesa? I just look for Studebaker's smoke signals....

salmon salad + grapefruit vinaigrette

serves 6 to 8 friends | as a main

At Gingham, we love smoke. You can smoke almost anything, and believe me, we do! This is a kind of smoky salad, with deep flavors of smoke in the salmon that are balanced by citrus, Mexican spices, sweet corn, and peppery arugula. This is a great dinner salad for eating al fresco on a warm summer night!

[for the salmon rub]
1 cup dark brown sugar
1 cup granulated sugar
1 cup kosher salt
1 teaspoon dill, dried
1 teaspoon oregano, dried
1 teaspoon thyme, fresh, picked
2 pounds fresh salmon, skin off and pinbones removed
Hickory chips, for smoking

[for the grapefruit vinaigrette]
¼ cup Champagne vinegar
2 tablespoons Dijon mustard
¼ cup freshly squeezed grapefruit juice
1 tablespoon grapefruit zest
2 tablespoons honey
1 tablespoon shallot, finely diced
2 sprigs thyme, leaves only
1½ cups canola or other neutral oil
Kosher salt and freshly ground black pepper, to taste

[for the salad]
8 teaspoons hominy (grits)
1 tablespoon canola oil
1 tablespoon (or more to taste) Tajin Mexican chile citrus spice (available at some supermarkets and Target)
6 to 8 large handfuls arugula
6 cups roasted corn, cut off the cob
4 cups roasted tomatoes, chopped (See recipe, page 93)
3 grapefruits, segmented
2 avocados, sliced or chopped

[how to do it]

Chef's note: Start this recipe a day ahead.

1. Make the rub: In a large bowl, combine all the ingredients, except the salmon.
2. Massage the salmon generously with the rub. Cover tightly in plastic wrap and refrigerate overnight.
3. Soak the wood chips. Preheat a grill or smoker to 140°F. Rinse the salmon and place it on a sheet tray. Smoke for 1 hour. Remove from heat and allow to cool to room temperature.
4. Make the vinaigrette: In a blender (or whisking by hand), combine all the ingredients except the oil. Drizzle the oil in a slow, steady stream to incorporate until emulsified. Adjust seasoning if necessary.
5. Start the salad: Fry the hominy in the oil until crispy and brown. Remove from heat and toss with the Tajin.
6. Assemble the salad: Toss the arugula with the cooked salmon flaked into pieces, corn, tomatoes, and grapefruit segments. Add the vinaigrette to taste.
7. To serve: Plate the salad and top each serving with hominy and avocado.

arugula salad + creamy anchovy dressing

serves 6 to 8 friends | as an app

The great thing about American classics is that they can be reinterpreted in so many ways. How do we do something familiar that we know everyone loves and then give it our own little twist? Here's Chef Ryan's take on Caesar salad, but done with a little "smokehouse cowboy attitude" thrown in. Big bold flavors, spicy, peppery arugula, smoky corn, and roasted tomatoes give this an extra heartiness that satisfies the wrangler in everyone!

[for the roasted tomatoes]
2 pounds Roma tomatoes, halved, stems removed
1 tablespoon olive oil
1 sprig thyme
5 cloves fresh garlic, minced or sliced thin
Kosher salt and freshly ground black pepper, to taste

[for the dressing]
1 egg yolk
1 salted anchovy, cleaned and diced small (Italian salt-packed is best)
1 clove fresh garlic, diced small
1 tablespoon red wine vinegar
1 teaspoon Worcestershire sauce
1 cup canola oil or an 80/20 olive oil blend
1 tablespoon freshly squeezed lemon juice
½ cup freshly grated Parmesan or Pecorino cheese
Freshly ground black pepper, to taste

[for the salad]
6 to 8 large handfuls baby arugula
1 cup sweet white corn, grilled first, then cut off the cob
½ cup freshly grated or shaved Pecorino cheese
Kosher salt and freshly ground black pepper, to taste

[how to do it]

1. Roast the tomatoes: Preheat a grill or oven to 300°F. In a bowl, gently toss together all the ingredients and season with salt and black pepper. Place the tomatoes on a sheet tray face up.
2. Roast until oven-dried, about 3 hours. Cool to room temperature before using, or store refrigerated, up to 6 days.
3. Make the dressing: Whisk together the egg yolk, anchovy, garlic, red wine vinegar, and Worcestershire sauce. In a slow, steady stream, whisk in the oil, adjusting consistency with cold water as needed. Finish with lemon juice and cheese. Add black pepper to taste.
4. Assemble the salad: In a large bowl, toss the arugula, corn, and tomatoes with dressing and seasoning according to your taste. Top with cheese, and serve.

smoked corn-off-the-cob

serves 4 to 6 friends | as a side

This dish is so popular, I know I'm going to regret giving you the secret to doing it yourself! We have some version of this on a few of our menus and not a single night goes by that I don't hear at least a dozen customers RAVE about it! It's not hard to do, it's just about combining a bunch of great flavors that go great together. I love to make this as a side for grilled salmon, albacore, or swordfish. When I have any of this leftover (almost never!) I use it as a side dish for a marinated flank steak or for breakfast with melted jack and a couple of fried eggs on top. Good morning, sunshine!

[for the corn cream]
1½ cups smoked sweet corn, cut off the cob
½ cup heavy cream
½ cup buttermilk
½ pasilla or poblano chile, seeded
¼ teaspoon cayenne powder
½ lime, zested and juiced
⅛ cup sour cream
Kosher salt and sugar, to taste

[for the corn]
2 tablespoons olive oil
1 cup chorizo, cut into ½-inch cubes
¼ cup red onion, diced
¼ cup jalapeño chile, seeded and diced
1 teaspoon fresh garlic, minced
4 cups sweet corn, cut off the cob
2 tablespoons unsalted butter
¼ cup cilantro leaves, roughly chopped
Kosher salt and freshly ground black pepper, to taste

[how to do it]

Chef's note: We use smoked corn for this recipe, because we are always down for extra smokiness. Most people, however, don't want to spend the time smoking corn. No worries: It still tastes great with plain sweet corn.

1. Make the cream: Place all ingredients, except lime juice and sour cream, in a medium saucepan. Bring the mixture to a gentle simmer and stir in the lime juice and sour cream. Remove from heat and let cool.
2. In a stand blender or with an immersion blender, process the mixture until smooth. Press through a mesh strainer, adjust seasoning, and set aside.
3. Make the corn: In a medium sauté pan, heat the oil to hot and sauté the chorizo briefly to render some of the fat.
4. Add the onion, jalapeño, and garlic, and sauté until soft. Add the corn and butter, and sauté until the corn begins to crackle. Stir in ½ cup of the cream, cilantro, and adjust seasoning with salt and pepper, if needed.
5. To serve: Pile high on your plate and enjoy!

"Chef Ryan's special smoky rub makes this dish spectacular. You should make a big batch of it, and just keep it around anytime you're going to grill anything!"

smoked baby back ribs + golden state bbq sauce

serves 6 to 8 friends | as a main

You want to get the best flavor from your rubs and marinades? Then you want them working for at least 8 to 10 hours ahead of time. The barbecue sauce we do with this is a kick-ass, mustard-based South Carolina-style joint. Tart, spicy, and sweet with a big splash of hefeweizen to keep it real!

[for the smoky rub]
½ cup paprika
½ cup kosher salt
½ cup dark brown sugar
2 teaspoons freshly ground black pepper
1 teaspoon white pepper
¼ cup garlic powder
¼ cup onion powder
1 teaspoon dark chile powder
1 teaspoon sage, dried
2 teaspoons ground cumin
1 teaspoon cayenne powder

[for the ribs]
4 racks baby back ribs, skinned
Water or apple juice
Hickory chips, for smoking

[for the bbq sauce]
2 tablespoons canola oil
1 yellow onion, diced
1½ cups hefeweizen or wheat beer
1½ cups apple cider vinegar
¼ cup honey
¼ cup dark brown sugar
2 tablespoons Worcestershire sauce
3 cups yellow mustard
Kosher salt and freshly ground black pepper, to taste

[how to do it]

Chef's note: This recipe requires minimum of 8 hours to cure the ribs in the rub. While the ribs are on the grill, thin out some of the barbecue sauce with a little corn stock, veg stock, or apple juice and use it as the "mop" to keep them moist.

1. Make the smoky rub: In a large bowl, thoroughly combine all the ingredients.
2. Massage the ribs with ample rub, wrap them tightly in plastic wrap, and place them in the refrigerator for a minimum of 8 hours (maximum 36 hours). (The extra rub will keep for 6 months at room temperature.)
3. Make the bbq sauce: In a medium saucepan, heat the oil to hot and sauté the onions until they become translucent. Deglaze the pan with the beer and the vinegar, and reduce by one-quarter.
4. Add the remaining ingredients and bring the mixture just to a boil. Remove from heat and in a stand blender (or an immersion blender) process until smooth. Press through a coarse strainer. (This recipe makes 4 cups of sauce, which will keep, refrigerated for up to 3 months.)
5. Preheat a grill or smoker to 225°F.
6. Cook the ribs: Smoke the ribs over hickory chips for a minimum of 2 hours, spraying them with the apple juice or water intermittently to keep them moist.
7. Reduce the heat to 175°F and smoke for an additional 1 to 2 hours.
8. Serve with Golden State BBQ sauce and fried brussels sprouts. (See recipe, page 104.)

shrimp + smoky oxtail grits

serves 4 friends | as an app

Get your Southern groove on for this one! We got Chef Ryan's grits with smoked and braised oxtail, shrimp, Cajun spices, roasted tomatoes, and a whole lotta good ol' Southern charm. If you've never done grits before, don't sweat it! They're easy and they give you a unique, creamy, chewy texture that is the perfect backdrop for the crazy complex flavors in this beautiful dish.

[for the oxtail]

Smoky rub (See recipe, page 97)
2 pounds oxtail, cut into 2-inch thick pieces (ask your butcher)
Kosher salt and freshly ground black pepper, to taste
Hickory chips, for smoking
3 to 4 cups beef stock

[for the roasted tomatoes]

2 pounds Roma tomatoes, halved, stems removed
1 tablespoon olive oil
1 sprig fresh thyme
1 clove fresh garlic, minced or sliced thin
Kosher salt and freshly ground black pepper, to taste

[for the shrimp]

2 tablespoons canola oil
1 pound raw shrimp (16 to 20 count), peeled and deveined
1 teaspoon fresh garlic, minced
2 tablespoons bourbon
2 tablespoons white wine
2 tablespoons vegetable stock or water
1 tablespoon Cajun seasoning (I like Tony Chachere's)
2 tablespoons butter
Kosher salt and freshly ground black pepper, to taste

[for the grits]

3½ cups vegetable stock (or smoked corn stock)
1 cup quick grits
1 cup smoked cheddar, shredded
2 tablespoons butter
¼ cup buttermilk
1 teaspoon Cajun seasoning
Kosher salt and freshly ground black pepper, to taste

[finishing touch]

Fresh chives or scallions, minced

[how to do it]

Chef's note: Start this dish 6 to 24 hours ahead of time.

1. Prepare the oxtail: Make the smoky rub. Season the meat with salt and pepper. Massage all the pieces generously with the rub and refrigerate overnight, or for a minimum of 6 hours. Preheat a smoker or a grill with hickory chips to 165°F. Smoke the oxtail for approximately 6 hours, or until it is fall-apart tender. Remove the meat from the smoker and cool slightly on a sheet tray. While still warm, remove the meat from the bone and discard any excess fat. Place on separate sheet tray to continue cooling.

2. Braise the oxtail: Preheat oven to 250°F. Place the oxtail in an ovenproof dish. In a medium stockpot, bring the stock to a boil and pour over the oxtail to cover completely. Put in the oven and cook for 2 to 3 hours.

3. Roast the tomatoes: Preheat a grill or oven to 300°F. In a bowl, gently toss together all the ingredients and season with salt and black pepper. Place the tomatoes on a baking pan face up. Roast until oven-dried, about 3 hours. Cool to room temperature before use, or store refrigerated.

4. Cook the shrimp: In a sauté pan, heat the oil to near smoking and cook the shrimp for 30 seconds. Add the oxtail, garlic, and 2 roasted tomatoes. Deglaze the pan with bourbon, wine, and stock or water. (Careful, the pan may flambé!) Allow the liquid to reduce and thicken to a sauce consistency, about 1 to 2 minutes. Stir in the Cajun seasoning and butter. Adjust the seasoning with salt and pepper, if needed, and set aside.

5. Make the grits: Bring the stock to a boil. Reduce the heat to low and whisk the grits in slowly. Simmer on low for 10 minutes, stirring frequently. Whisk in the remaining ingredients and adjust seasoning as necessary.

6. To serve: Portion the grits into serving bowls and top each with a generous amount of the shrimp mixture.

tri-tip sandwich + sautéed mushrooms + jalapeño jam

serves 4 friends | as a main

So here's how we imagine it: A guy from Philly walks into a Texas sandwich shop and asks for a cheesesteak. After the guffaws die down, this is what they hand him — smoky beef slathered in a sweet-and-spicy jalapeño jam and rich, creamy baconnaise. Adorned with mushrooms and a Gruyère with attitude, this is how we do sandwiches in the land of the lone star!

[for the tri-tip]
2 to 3 pounds beef tri-tip
Smoky rub (See recipe, page 97)
Hickory chips, for smoking

[for the jalapeño jam]
2 tablespoons vegetable oil
1 pound yellow onion, diced
½ pound jalapeño chiles, half seeded and ribbed, half with seeds
2 tablespoons fresh garlic, chopped
1 teaspoon granulated sugar
¼ cup golden balsamic vinegar (or cider vinegar)
1 tablespoon fresh thyme leaves
2 tablespoons canola oil

[for the baconnaise]
2 egg yolks
½ cup bacon fat
1 tablespoon malt vinegar
1 tablespoon freshly squeezed lemon juice
1½ cups canola oil
1 tablespoon cold water
Kosher salt, to taste

[for the mushrooms]
2 tablespoons canola oil
1 pound cremini mushrooms, sliced about ⅛-inch thin
1 tablespoon thyme leaves
1 tablespoon butter

[finishing touches]
½ pound Gruyère cheese, sliced
4 soft hoagie rolls, toasted

[how to do it]

Chef's note: Start this recipe 8 to 24 hours ahead of time. Also, this recipe makes more jalapeño jam and baconnaise than you'll need, but you can use these condiments for a ton of other stuff.

1. Prepare the meat: Massage the tri-tip with the rub, cover tightly in plastic wrap, and refrigerate for a minimum of 8 hours and a maximum of 24 hours.
2. Make the jam: In a medium sauté pan, heat the vegetable oil and cook the onions until tender. Add the jalapeño and garlic and cook until tender. Add the sugar, vinegar, and thyme. Simmer and reduce until about three-quarters of the liquid evaporates. Remove from heat and allow to cool a bit. Place the jam mixture in a food processor or blender, and add the canola oil in a slow, steady stream until smooth.
3. Cook the tri-tip: Preheat a smoker or a grill with hickory chips to 150°F. Cook until tri-tip reaches an internal temperature of 135°F, about 1 to 1½ hours. Remove from heat and allow the meat to rest for 20 minutes before refrigerating. Slice the beef once it is completely cooled, and reserve the juices. Quickly sauté the slices in some of the meat juices (think cheesesteak technique here) with mushrooms, then top with cheese until just melted.
4. Make the baconnaise: In a blender, combine the yolks, bacon fat, vinegar, and lemon juice. Drizzle the oil in a slow steady stream, alternating with water to emulsify. (If the yolks and oil get too thick the mayo will break, so use a couple of drops of water to thin it out and keep it moving nicely.) Taste and adjust seasoning as necessary.
5. Sauté the mushrooms: In a large sauté pan, get the oil very hot. Add the mushrooms and sauté until slightly browned. Add the thyme, and salt and pepper to taste. Swirl in the butter to melt and coat. Remove from heat.
6. To serve: Slather rolls with jam on one side and baconnaise on the other. Top with tri-tip and cheese.

beer-braised lamb shanks

serves 8 friends | as a main

This is Chef Ryan's "French-influenced menu item" for Gingham. Lamb is a popular meat on French menus, and the braise is a traditional cooking technique — but we're not traditional! So we put our own spin on it and added the chiles and the beer to give it a special kick and to bring it around to more of a barbecue-influenced kind of braise. When this comes out of the roasting pan, the meat should fall right off the bone. And when it hits your mouth, it will simply melt into fatty, spicy, citrus deliciousness! A couple of bottles of cold hefeweizen are all you need!

[for the lamb]

8 lamb foreshanks
Kosher salt and freshly ground black pepper, to taste
1 bunch fresh thyme
1 orange, zested and juiced
1 to 3 Fresno chiles, minced, to taste
6 tablespoons canola oil, divided use
8 cups mirepoix (roughly chopped carrots, celery, and onion)
¾ cup fresh garlic, smashed
½ cup tomato paste
24 ounces hefeweizen (or other wheat beer)
6 ounces freshly squeezed orange juice
16 cups (4 quarts) chicken stock
16 cups (4 quarts) vegetable stock

[finishing touch]

Gremolata (4 tablespoons chopped fresh parsley, 2 tablespoons chopped fresh garlic, and 2 tablespoons grated orange zest, combined)

[how to do it]

Chef's note: This recipe is best started a day in advance. Recipe can be cut in half to serve 4.

1. Season the lamb shanks with salt, pepper, thyme, orange zest, Fresno chiles, and 4 tablespoons of vegetable oil, and refrigerate covered overnight.
2. Preheat oven to 300°F.
3. Wipe the herbs, orange, and chiles from the shanks. In a large sauté pan, heat the remaining oil to hot and sear the shanks on all sides. As each one is seared, place it in a large ovenproof roasting pan.
4. Add the mirepoix to the sauté pan and cook until the vegetables are browned and caramelized, about 10 to 15 minutes.
5. Add the garlic to the pan and sweat until cooked through. Stir in the tomato paste and sauté briefly.
6. Add the beer and orange juice and reduce by one-third. Pour the mirepoix mixture into a large stockpot, add the stocks, and bring to a boil.
7. Pour the liquid into the roasting pan to cover the lamb. Cover with foil or parchment paper and cook in the oven for 3 hours, or until the meat is fork-tender and pulls away easily from the bone.
8. Serve lamb shanks topped with gremolata and a starch of your choice (I love to serve it with grits).

gingham's fried brussels sprouts

serves 6 to 8 friends | as a app or side

Here's the Gingham riff on brussels. Deep-fried goodness with the zip of jalapeño and anchovy, all topped off with some smoky, crunchy almonds. Make a bunch extra, because once they're done, you'll be popping them in your mouth and you won't be able to stop. Make sure you leave enough for your friends!

[for the dressing]
1 cup apple cider vinegar
½ cup honey
2 salt-packed anchovies, rinsed and minced
1 cup jalapeño chiles, seeded and minced
½ cup fresh garlic, minced
Kosher salt and freshly ground black pepper, to taste

[for the brussels]
Canola oil, for frying
2 pounds brussels sprouts, stems trimmed and cut in half

[finishing touches]
½ cup smoked almonds, crushed
Kosher salt, to taste

[how to do it]

1. **Make the dressing:** In a medium bowl, whisk together all the dressing ingredients until smooth. Set aside.
2. **Cook the brussels:** In a large pan, heat oil to very hot (near smoking) and fry the brussels until crispy, about 1 to 2 minutes. (BE CAREFUL. They will pop! A splatter screen is strongly recommended.)
3. Drain the the brussels sprouts on paper towels, then toss them with the dressing, smoked almonds, and salt to taste.

bacon + chive waffles + bourbon-rosemary syrup

serves 2 to 4 friends | makes about 6 large Belgian-style waffles

For my breakfasts, pork is king! Here's a way to combine the homey deliciousness of from-scratch batter with the salty, sweet goodness of bacon. And why waste that bacon fat, filled with rich, smoky, fatty flavor? Sub some of it in the batter for canola oil! And then on top — bourbon and maple syrup. The perfect breakfast sauce! Get outta bed and come get your Sunday started with this!

[for the syrup]
½ cup bourbon
1 cup dark brown sugar
½ cup water
2 cups pure maple syrup
1 sprig fresh rosemary

[for the batter]
2 eggs
2 cups milk
1½ cups buttermilk
½ cup canola oil
6 strips bacon, cooked crisp and crumbled (reserve 2 tablespoons warm bacon fat)
½ teaspoon pure vanilla extract
2 cups all-purpose flour
2 tablespoons baking powder
3 tablespoons fresh chives, chopped
1 teaspoon granulated sugar
2 cups cheddar cheese, shredded (do NOT add to batter until cooking!)

[how to do it]

1. Make the syrup: In a medium saucepan on medium heat, flambé the bourbon and reduce by half. Stir in the sugar and water, and cook on low until it reaches a syrup consistency. Add the maple syrup and rosemary and bring the temperature up to just below a boil. Remove from heat, and let steep with the rosemary while cooling. Strain and store at room temperature until ready for use. (This recipe makes 1 quart of syrup that will keep covered at room temperature for up to 6 months.)
2. Make the batter: In a small bowl, whisk together the egg, milks, canola oil, bacon fat, and vanilla.
3. In a medium bowl, stir together the flour, baking powder, bacon, chives, and sugar.
4. Add the egg mixture to the dry mixture and whisk together to combine well.
5. Heat a waffle iron. For each waffle, pour some batter onto the iron and add a little less than ¼ cup cheddar to the top of the batter before closing the lid.
6. When each waffle has reached maximum crispy deliciousness, pull it off the iron and serve it immediately with the bourbon syrup!

"This recipe was inspired by the home cooking I had as a kid, especially breakfasts from scratch with my granddad, Dewey Gould."
— Chef Ryan

gaba

rdine

AS IF THINGS WEREN'T MOVING FAST ENOUGH AFTER THE SUCCESSES OF SEARSUCKER,

Burlap, and Gingham, James calls me up and says he's identified a great building in Point Loma, in a great little neighborhood. It's also the quintessential San Diego spot: Near the water, you can smell the ocean everywhere, and there's always sailboats and seagulls within sight. This space was much smaller and much cuter than anything we had done before, but there was a definite charm in that. Where the other restaurants were big floor plans ("social dining" nightspots with couches and DJs), this was a comfy little 88-seater. And this being a smaller venue, with a smaller kitchen, I realized this was my opportunity to get back into the kitchen myself, to roll up my sleeves, and to do some hands-on cooking for a while. I wanted a place where I could get back to touching the food, having fun with the other chefs on the line, getting my hands dirty again. Being so close to the ocean, it was clear that this place would be all about local seafood, with a great raw bar and all kinds of fish that come in fresh off the boats every day. It's just down the hill from my house, so it's also the comfortable neighborhood place where one day my own kids will be washing dishes and bussing tables. How did we come up with this name, you ask? Gabardine was a fabric that was created by Burberry in the late 1800s for use by fishermen and in nautical environments. It was very weatherproof, rain resistant, holds up to wind, and now it's a fine gentleman's suit. So we liked the idea of a fabric that had been used by working people in a rough, natural ocean setting that has evolved into something more refined, but still maintains its casual charm. We're fond of saying that Gabardine is a great place to GAB, BAR, and DINE.

GABARDINE

tuna salsa

serves 4 friends | as an app

This is our playful twist on "poke or tartar," but instead of Asian, we made our tuna very South-by-Southwest. In the restaurants, we have a lot of tuna belly and tuna that we scrape from the skin — this is some of the fattiest and most flavorful meat on the fish. You can also simply buy some nice albacore tuna and dice it up. (We prefer to use albacore "white" tuna as it is very sustainable and very affordable!)

[for the salsa]
2 Roma tomatoes, seeded and diced
½ red onion, diced
1 ear yellow corn, cut off the cob
1 tablespoon cilantro, minced
1 tablespoon Sriracha (or other hot sauce)
1 tablespoon olive oil
1 lime, zested and juiced
Kosher salt and freshly ground black pepper, to taste
½ pound albacore tuna steak, diced

[finishing touch]
Fried tortillas or tortilla chips

[how to do it]

1. In a large bowl, thoroughly mix all the ingredients, except the tuna. Gently fold in the tuna until just combined (don't over handle the tuna or it will get "cloudy").
2. Serve with fried tortillas or chips!

"Keep that Sriracha handy and feel free to take the heat up a few notches. The more personality this dish has, the more fun your guests will have. No one wants an ordinary dish, they want an extraordinary dish!! Go for it!!!"

'summer loving' watermelon salad

serves 4 friends | as an app

I'm a SoCal guy — I love the sand, surf, and sea, and I love crisp, cold, refreshing salads you can dig into when it's hot and you're fried from being out soaking up sun all day. This recipe combines the crispiness of lettuce with the cold sweetness of watermelon and tomatoes to make one satisfying summer salad. Serve it up and feel the love!

[for the balsamic syrup]
1 cup balsamic vinegar
¼ cup granulated sugar

[for the vinaigrette]
1 cup sherry vinegar
¼ cup honey
½ red onion, diced
½ cup extra virgin olive oil
Kosher salt and freshly ground black pepper, to taste

[for the salad]
1 big handful spring mixed greens
4 cups red and yellow seedless watermelon, diced large
3 cups Capri tomatoes, diced large or red and yellow cherry or pear tomatoes, sliced in half
1 tablespoon chives, sliced into thin strips
6 fresh basil leaves, sliced into thin strips
⅓ cup goat cheese

[finishing touch]
Edible flowers (optional)

[how to do it]

Chef's note: This balsamic syrup can be used for a ton of things. It's great as a garnish for everything from grilled chicken to ice cream to watermelon salad.

1. Make the balsamic syrup: In a small saucepot over medium heat combine the balsamic and sugar and reduce by about half until it just reaches a syrup consistency. (Note: you can flavor the balsamic with everything from blackberries to cherries to orange to bacon to figs — let your imagination go crazy!)
2. Make the vinaigrette: In a small saucepot bring the sherry vinegar and honey to a boil. Add the onion and turn the heat off. Let cool to room temperature, about 1 hour, and strain out the pickled onions (save them for the salad).
3. Assemble and serve: In a large bowl, whisk together half the sherry mixture with the olive oil (save the rest for another day). Taste and adjust seasoning. Toss in all the salad ingredients, except for the goat cheese, and mix well to combine and coat with dressing. Crumble the goat cheese over the top, garnish with edible flowers, if desired, and finish with a drizzle bomb of balsamic syrup all over!

spicy tomato + cucumber salad

serves 4 friends | as an app

I love the seeds of cucumbers and even more of tomatoes (find the ripest you can!). The color of cucumber skin, as well as the texture, is super appealing, especially for a cool, fresh salad like this one — so make peel strips! Half peeled and half not. This simple salad is meant to be "unapologetically" HOT! So if you aren't saying sorry after the first bite, add more HEAT!!!

[for the salad]

1 cucumber, half peeled, sliced down the middle, cut in half moons
3 Roma or Capri tomatoes, cut into similar size as cucumber
1 handful arugula (or other spicy greens, such as mizuna or mustard)

[for the vinaigrette]

1 tablespoon Sambal or Sriracha chile paste
2 tablespoons soy sauce
1 lime, zested and juiced
3 tablespoons extra virgin olive oil
Kosher salt and freshly ground black pepper, to taste

[how to do it]

1. **Assemble the salad:** In a large bowl, combine all the salad ingredients.
2. **Make the vinaigrette:** In a medium bowl, whisk together the chile paste, soy sauce, and lime juice and zest. Add the olive oil in a slow steady stream while whisking. Taste and season with salt and pepper.
3. **To serve:** You can add the tomatoes and cucumbers to the vinaigrette 10 to 20 minutes before serving as a little pre-marinade! When ready to serve, toss in the spicy greens, grab a cold bottle of beer, sake, or white wine, and it's show time!

b.l.a.t

serves 4 friends | as an app

This salad is what I call the "man" salad. It's the salad that tries to be too much and is overdressed! Big and bold, filled with sharp, mouth-filling flavors, this is a salad that can stand up to anything and can even be a meal if you make enough! Roll up your sleeves, and load up your fork!

[for the chipotle and buttermilk dressing]

2 tablespoons chipotle chiles in adobo
2 tablespoons freshly squeezed lemon juice
½ cup mayonnaise
½ cup buttermilk
1 handful fresh Italian parsley
Kosher salt and freshly ground black pepper, to taste

[for the salad]

2 handfuls mixed leafy greens, chopped large
2 heads baby romaine lettuce, sliced lengthwise and charred on a grill
3 heirloom or vine-ripened tomatoes, cubed
2 avocados, diced or sliced
4 to 6 strips bacon, cooked crispy
1 handful blue cheese, crumbled

[how to do it]

1. Make the dressing: In a blender, combine all the ingredients and blend until smooth. Taste and adjust seasoning if necessary. (If the dressing is too thick, add a little water to thin it out. I like this dressing to stand up and not be to "cutesy." Think "big and bold!") Refrigerate until ready to use.

2. Assemble and serve: In a salad bowl add the lettuce, top with a layer of tomatoes, then topped with avocados. Pour on the dressing (be overly generous!), and toss to distribute and coat the lettuce. Top that with bacon and finish with crumbled blue cheese. Taste what you have, and season with salt and pepper.

oysters on the half shell

serves 1 to 2 friends | as an app

I consider a great fresh oyster to be one of nature's most perfect foods. These little lumps of briny deliciousness are like tasting the entire ocean all compacted into one bite. I call oysters the "original aphrodisiacs," and — like most sexy things — you shouldn't have to do too much to them to make them attractive! Here's my simple mignonette recipe — the classic accompaniment. If it's the middle of summer, and it's hot, and you're feeling especially lazy, a simple squirt of lemon will also do just fine!

[for the strawberry and champagne mignonette]
1 plump, ripe strawberry, finely diced
½ medium to large shallot, finely minced
2 tablespoons Champagne vinegar
¼ teaspoon cracked black pepper or pink peppercorns
1 dozen oysters, freshly shucked, on ice or rock salt

[how to do it]

Chef's note: Here's enough mignonette to do a dozen oysters. You can easily scale up the ingredients, depending on how many friends are eating these. I usually figure on 6 to 12 per person.

1. In a medium bowl, gently whisk together all the ingredients and let it sit for about 10 minutes. Put about a half teaspoon on top of each oyster, close your eyes, and savor.

"To eat an oyster is to kiss a mermaid on the lips."
—James Joyce

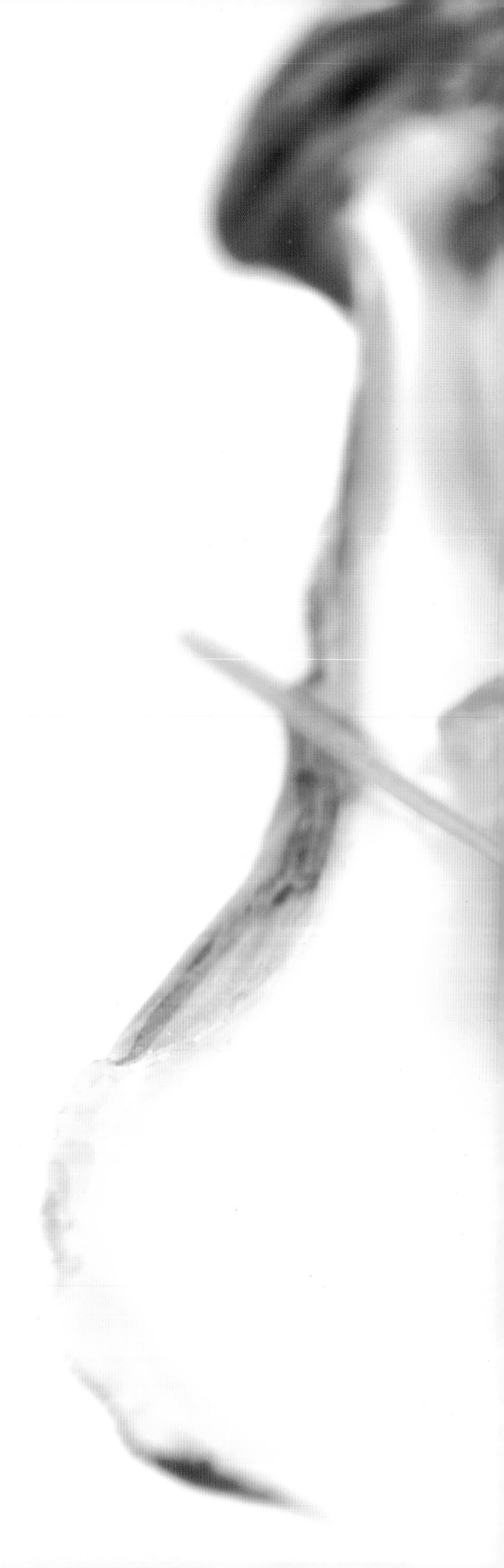

maine scallops + sautéed corn + frank's butter sauce

serves 4 friends | as an app

I love to cook dishes that are simple to prepare, don't take much time, don't use up every piece of equipment in my kitchen, and yet deliver awesome flavor. You can do this entire dish in one large sauté pan, and you only need to cook each of the components for a few minutes. What you have when you're done is a great combination of sweet, salty, spicy, buttery goodness that will make you break into a grin from ear to ear (that's because it's got corn in it!). Too corny?

[for the scallops]
1 to 2 tablespoons canola oil
12 to 20 scallops (U-8, the big boys), about 3 to 5 per person
¼ stick (1 ounce) butter
1 lemon, zested and juiced
Kosher salt and freshly ground black pepper, to taste

[for the corn]
1 tablespoon canola oil
¼ stick (1 ounce) butter
½ red onion, minced
2 teaspoons fresh garlic, minced
2 ears fresh yellow corn, kernels removed and reserved
Squeeze fresh lemon
1 teaspoon fresh cilantro, minced

[for the beurre blanc]
¼ stick (1 ounce) butter
1 tablespoon Frank's Red Hot sauce
¼ cup white wine

[finishing touches]
Italian parsley leaves
Pea shoots

[how to do it]

Chef's note: Two keys to great scallop cooking. 1. You always want a dry scallop for sauté, so make sure you pat them dry before putting them in a hot pan. 2. Make sure there's enough room in the pan; don't overcrowd them (they shouldn't be touching). Cook in two separate pans, or in batches, if you need to.

1. Cook the scallops: In a large sauté pan, heat the oil to very hot (almost smoking). Lay the scallops in and let them sit, undisturbed, for about 1 minute. (Here's where you develop that brown, crunchy crust that you want on them.) Flip them over, hit them with the butter, baste it on there as it melts, and squeeze some lemon juice over them. Take them out of the pan and let them rest on a plate (they will release some of their juices).
2. Make the corn: In the hot pan on medium-high, heat the oil and melt the butter. Sauté the onion and garlic until nicely caramelized, and add the corn, and cook for a minute or so. Squeeze a little lemon in, add the cilantro, and stir. Remove the corn mixture from the pan.
3. Make the beurre blanc: To the pan, add the butter and melt. Add the hot sauce and wine and whisk together well. Continue whisking until the mixture thickens and lightens.
4. To serve: Place a bed of corn on each plate and top with scallops. Spoon the beurre blanc over the scallops and garnish with the greens of your choosing.

clam pasta

serves 4 friends | as a main

Yes, yes, yes! It's been done before but it's so good you have to do it again and again — and this time you can make it better than you ever have before! Get creative. Have fun. For mushrooms, find some nice chanterelles, hen of the woods, porcini, morels, or shiitakes if you can. Like peppers? Dice up some red or orange bell peppers and throw 'em on in. If you've got a spicy personality, flip in some diced chiles like Anaheims, pasillas, or banana peppers. Go out to your garden or local farmers market and grab some zucchini, onions, tomatoes — you can throw almost anything in this one!

1 big handful (about 1 pound) dried fettucine
½ stick (2 ounces) butter
2 tablespoons extra virgin olive oil
4 strips bacon or pancetta, diced
4 cloves fresh garlic, sliced
2 handfuls great fresh mushrooms, quartered or diced
24 clams, rinsed well (Manila or similar)
1 cup white wine
1 lemon, zested and juiced
¼ bunch fresh parsley, chopped
1 pinch red chile flakes
Kosher salt and freshly ground black pepper, to taste

[finishing touches]

Freshly grated Parmesan cheese
Crusty bread to soak up that winey garlic-lemon love!

[how to do it]

1. Bring a medium saucepot filled with water and a couple drops of olive oil to a boil. Drop the pasta in as the butter hits the sauté pan.
2. In a large sauté pan on high heat, melt the butter and extra virgin olive oil and add the diced bacon. When the bacon starts to crisp, add the garlic and mushrooms. Sauté until the mushrooms have given up their liquid and start to brown.
3. Now add the clams. (It's time to roll that wrist!) Coat the clams in the bacon-garlic-mushroom love! After a minute or so, hit the pan with the white wine and cover with a lid, another sauté pan, or some foil.
4. Cook, covered, for about 8 to 10 minutes, or until the clams pop open (discard any unopened ones).
5. Add the cooked pasta to the pan, along with the lemon zest, lemon juice, parsley, chile flakes, and salt and pepper.
6. To serve: Stir, taste, and garnish with the Parmesan so your friends can get their cheese on! Pair with that nice chardonnay or that lovely Sancerre you sacrificed to the "gods" of the sauté pan.

"I love this dish on a lazy Sunday
afternoon. It screams for cold white
wine, like a great pinot grigio or a
New Zealand sauvignon blanc!"

ez eat shrimp

serves 4 friends | as an app

Who wants to "peel and eat" when you can make it so much more enjoyable for your friends to get right to it without the mess and fuss of peeling. This recipe is Gabardine's special twist on shrimp scampi. How did we come up with it? Well, we follow one of the cooking commandments: garlic, lemon, and butter make EVERYTHING taste better!

[for the shrimp]

½ stick (2 ounces) butter
16 shrimp (16 to 20 count), cleaned
1 to 2 tablespoons fresh garlic, chopped
¼ cup white wine
1 tablespoon fresh parsley, chopped
1 lemon, zested and juiced
Kosher salt and freshly ground black pepper, to taste

[finishing touch]

Grilled crusty bread (for soaking up the "love")

[how to do it]

1. In a large sauté pan over super high heat, add the butter and let it brown for about 1½ minutes. Add the shrimp. (The key here is to let them sit and get some great color on them — don't shake the pan!) After a minute, flip the shrimp and add the garlic. Cook for a minute or so, until the garlic gets some color.
2. Deglaze the pan with white wine (scraping any solids to dissolve and give you deliciousness). Add the parsley, zest, lemon juice, and season with salt and pepper. BAM! You're done! Fast and full of flavor! Serve with grilled bread.

baja mussels

serves 4 friends | as an app

This dish is summer in a bowl! (Does that make sense? It's a "dish" that's a "bowl"?) Well, anyway, this prep is a super easy way to cook mussels. Great food doesn't have to take a long time. Sometimes, the cleanest, simplest, fastest technique gives you the cleanest, freshest flavors! And you don't have to plan hours in advance for this! Fire up the pans, grab your butter, white wine, and lemon, and get it going!

[for the mussels]
½ stick (2 ounces) butter
2 Roma tomatoes, quartered
1 cup white wine
20 black or green mussels, rinsed and debearded
1 lemon, zested and juiced
2 tablespoons fresh parsley, chopped
2 tablespoons basil pesto (See recipe, page 33)
Kosher salt and freshly ground black pepper, to taste

[finishing touch]
Grilled crusty bread (for sauce-soaking!)

[how to do it]

1. Here's a super easy way to cook mussels! Get two sauté pans that are similar in size and big enough to hold the mussels. Heat one pan on medium-high heat to melt the butter. Add the tomatoes and sauté for 1 minute.
2. Add the white wine and mussels and cover with the second sauté pan, face down. Cook, covered, for 6 to 8 minutes.
3. Pull the top pan off. Your mussels should all be open (discard any that aren't). With a slotted spoon, transfer the mussels to a serving bowl (keep as much of the cooking liquid in the pan as possible).
4. Stir the lemon juice, zest, parsley, and pesto into the liquid left in the pan. Taste. Does it need more butter or white wine? Throw some more in! Season with salt and pepper, pour the sauce into the serving bowl, and grab a handful of that grilled bread!

maine lobster risotto

serves 4 friends | as a main

This is a great recipe with a bunch of steps. It takes a little time, but one forkful in your mouth and you'll know it was all worth it. You don't have to do it this way, but why are you looking at this cookbook if you don't want to go for it?! Put your apron on — this could get a little messy. Now, roll up your sleeves, pour yourself something cold, and get ready to do the lobster dance!

[for the lobsters and corn]
2 (2-pound) live Maine lobsters
2 lemons, cut in half
1 head fresh garlic, cut in half crosswise
2 ears fresh corn, shucked

[for the risotto]
1 tablespoon olive oil
1 large shallot, diced
1 cup Arborio rice
1 cup white wine
1 pinch fresh tarragon, finely chopped
½ stick (2 ounces) butter
½ cup freshly grated Parmesan cheese
Kosher salt and freshly ground black pepper, to taste

[finishing touches}
Freshly grated Parmesan cheese
Microgreens
Pea shoots
Basil pesto (See recipe, page 33) or pistou (a simple mash of basil, garlic, oil, with salt and pepper).

[how to do it]

1. Prepare the lobsters: Start the party by bringing a big pot of water to a boil (enough to cover two "unhappy" lobsters). Add the lemons and garlic, and season with just a little salt. Throw the lobsters into the pot and — wham bam! — they're off to lobster heaven. In 10 minutes those red little bugs are ready to shock in an ice bath! Get a big bowl of ice and water ready in the meantime. After you've taken the lobsters out and submerged them in the ice bath, add the corn to the lobster water and cook for about 3 minutes. Throw the corn in the water bath with the lobsters. Chill for a minute or so (that means you, too!).
2. Remove the lobsters and corn from the ice bath. Snap, Crackle, and Pop those lobsters open (if you're not sure how to do this, flip to the next page, where Burlap Chef Anthony gives the master class with photos).
3. When you've gotten all the meat from your lobsters, throw all the shells back into the boiling cooking liquid. Cut all the kernels of corn off the cob and save them, then throw the cobs back into the cooking liquid. Turn the heat up to high and bring the liquid back to a boil. Cook until it has reduced by at least one-third.
4. Cut the lobster up into cubes or nice bite-size pieces and add it to the corn. Set aside.
5. Start the risotto: Here's where it all starts to come together: In a large sauté pan over medium heat, get the olive oil hot and add the shallot and the rice. Sauté for about 4 minutes. Add the white wine and continue to stir. (The key to risotto is continuous stirring with a wooden spoon and a wine glass that will need to be refilled several times along the way!) Stir until the wine has disappeared.
6. Strain the lobster-corn broth. Start ladling it in to the rice, one ladle at a time. Stir until the liquid is absorbed and then — you got it — add another ladle of liquid. Repeat this until the risotto starts to become tender.
7. Fold in the lobster, corn, tarragon, butter, and some of the cheese. Add a little more stock and a little more cheese (come on, feel your groove!). Once the rice "creams" (when the rice releases its starch), taste it and adjust your final seasoning. You can add a little more liquid if you like, depending on your desired consistency. I like my risotto a little looser in the pot because it thickens as it cools on the plate. However you like it, the universal agreement is that you MUST eat it hot and NOW!
8. To serve: Garnish with a little Parmesan, microgreens, pea sprouts, arugula, or something green and fun. I like to serve it with a little basil pesto or pistou (a simple mash of basil, garlic, oil, with salt and pepper). Pull a few bottles of great chardonnay or sauvignon blanc from the fridge and pour yourself a big glass. You earned it! Exhale and mangia!!!

how to break down a lobster

Chef Anthony shows you that cooking and breaking down a lobster is not difficult, but there is a little technique involved. All you really need for tools are a sharp chef's knife and a few clean towels.

[1] Ten minutes in the pot, and the lobster should be done…

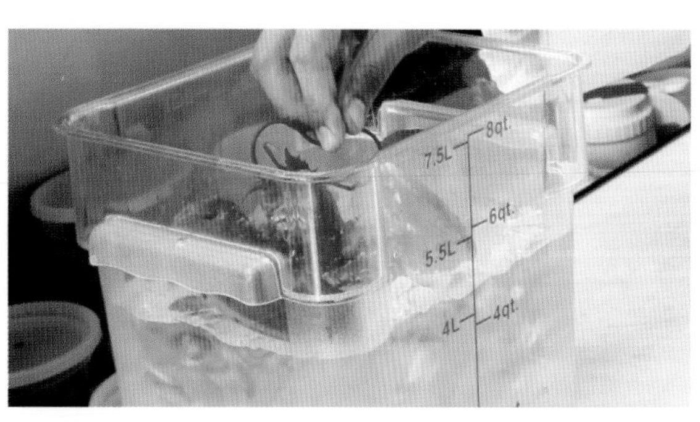

[2] Go from pot to ice bath right away, to stop the cooking and cool for handling.

[3] Hold the lobster body in one hand and twist off the claws with the other hand.

[4] To remove the tail, bend the body back and pull apart.

[5] Crack the shell on each claw with a knife...

[6] Open the claw at the crack and pull apart to free the meat inside.

[7] Try not to just pop the whole piece of claw meat into your mouth...

[8] To open the tail, make an incision on the bottom, then roll the tail in a towel.

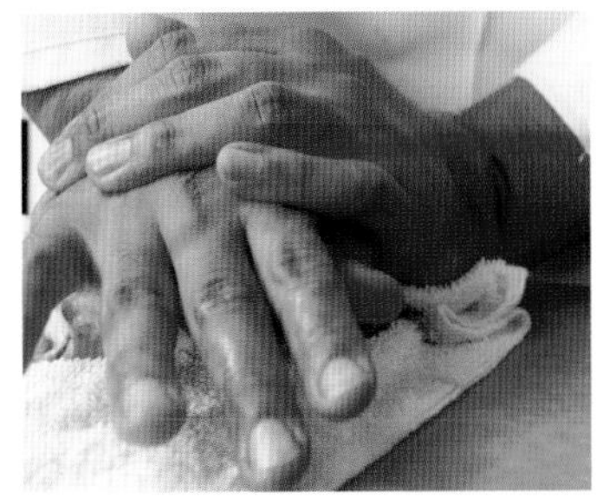

[9] Press down hard to crack the shell.

[10] When you unroll the towel, the tail meat should be easily freed.

[11] Trim up the tail meat and you're ready to use it!

top of the sir loin + cognac-peppercorn sauce + blue mashed potatoes

serves 4 friends | as a main

This is a classic combination of flavors and ingredients, inspired by the Great American Steakhouse. The cream-based brandy sauce has its roots in the typical au poivre sauce you've had a million times. And my old-style mashed potatoes (I don't even take the skins off, 'cause that's how I roll) and crispy onions complete the dish. To drink with this, you want a beverage with some muscle. A peppery syrah, a bold cabernet, a spicy zinfandel for a red wine, or you can go with some beer heavyweights, like a dopplebock, barleywine, or a Belgian-style dubbel, trippel, or quad.

[for the sauce]
1 tablespoon canola oil
1 shallot, diced
½ cup brandy (or whiskey or bourbon)
1 tablespoon beef demi-glace (available at Whole Foods, specialty food stores, and online)
1 cup heavy cream
1 heaping tablespoon green peppercorns

[for the mashed potatoes]
½ pound Yukon Gold potatoes
½ cup heavy cream
½ stick (2 ounces) butter
1 handful blue cheese, crumbled
Kosher salt and freshly ground black pepper, to taste

[for the onion strings]
1 large yellow or Spanish onion, sliced into thin rounds
¼ cup buttermilk
1 cup all-purpose flour
1 cup cornstarch
Kosher salt and freshly ground black pepper, to taste
2 cups canola oil, for frying

[for the steak]
1 (2-pound) sirloin, baseball cut (or filet, or any nice steak)
Kosher salt and freshly ground black pepper, to taste
Fresh Italian parsley, chopped
1 to 2 radishes, sliced thin

[how to do it]

1. Make the sauce: In a medium saucepan, heat the oil and add the shallot, cooking to a nice dark caramelization. Add ½ cup brandy (Stand back! It will flame up. Save your eyebrows!) and let it burn off about halfway. Add the heavy cream and the demi-glace and stir to melt and mix. Reduce by half again, until it thickens and can coat the back of a wooden spoon. Add the green peppercorns, stir for a minute or so, and taste. Adjust seasoning if necessary.
2. Make the potatoes: In a medium pot with salted water, bring the potatoes to a rolling boil and cook until very soft. Strain and transfer to a mixer with a paddle attachment (or a bowl using a hand masher) and smash the potatoes up with the cream and butter. (They should be really creamy, sexy, and loose.) Stir in the blue cheese. Taste and adjust seasoning if necessary. Keep warm.
3. Make the onions: Soak the sliced onions in buttermilk for 20 minutes. In a medium bowl, whisk together the flour and cornstarch until well combined. Season with salt and pepper.
4. Preheat a deep fryer or oil in a sauté pan to 350°F.
5. Coat the onions with the flour and cornstarch mix. Fry the onions until golden brown. Remove them from the oil and lay them on paper towels to drain and stay crispy.
6. Cook the steak: Preheat a grill on high. Season the meat with salt and a very generous amount of pepper. Grill

to medium rare (internal temperature of 135°F). Transfer to a platter, cover with foil, and let rest for at least 5 minutes before cutting into thick slices

7. To serve: Create a bed of mashed potatoes and top with steak slices. Douse the meat with a nice portion of sauce, sprinkle with parsley, and lay in a small handful of crispy onions right next door. Toss in a few slices of fresh radish as a garnish (there's the healthy ingredient!).

"Grilled sirloin. Blue cheese. Mashed potatoes. Peppercorns. Fried onions. When you eat this dish, you should move into a room with dark wood paneling and red velvet chairs! I can almost smell the cigar smoke!"

grilled pork chops + peach bbq sauce

serves 4 friends | as a main

Ever since we opened Gingham, we convinced ourselves that we can be good ol' boys, just barbecuing every damn thang. This sauce is just our excuse to do something with bourbon and peaches. It was inspired by the kitchen at Gingham in the summer, when we all like to drink our brown liquor and eat our fresh, ripe summer peaches. Pork, peaches, and bourbon — yow. A match made in ... purgatory!

[for the sauce]
1 tablespoon canola oil
½ yellow onion, diced
¼ cup fresh garlic, diced
1 jalapeño, chopped (seeds and all)
6 ripe peaches, divided use
½ cup bourbon
½ cup apple cider vinegar
1 cup chicken stock
1 tablespoon honey
½ stick (2 ounces) butter
1 tablespoon fresh Italian parsley, chopped (optional)

[for the pork]
4 thick-cut pork chops
Kosher salt and freshly ground black pepper, to taste

[finishing touch]
Cheesy grits (See recipe, page 98)

[how to do it]

1. Make the sauce: In a medium saucepot on high, heat the oil and add the onion and garlic. Sauté until they become translucent, about 3 minutes. Throw in the jalapeño, and sauté for a minute or two.
2. Rough chop 4 peaches (reserve the 2 nicest-looking ones) and throw them into the saucepot. Stir, cooking, for 2 to 3 minutes. Add the bourbon and deglaze. (Be careful of the flame! You should be able to dissolve some of the caramelization from the onions and garlic — a lot of flavor going on there!). Add the vinegar and then the chicken stock. Turn heat down to low simmer, add the honey, and reduce by half. Strain and return to a saucepot to simmer until needed.
3. Cook the pork: Preheat a grill to high. Grill the pork until the meat is firm and cooked through. Cut the reserved peaches in quarters and put them on the grill to get them nicely marked and caramelized.
4. Just before you're ready to serve, turn the sauce back up to high, add the butter and whisk it in. Finish with the Italian parsley, if desired.
5. To serve: Spoon a portion of grits on a plate, if desired. Top with pork chop, peach quarters and a generous ladle of sauce.

little chicken + "hot bread" salad + broken balsamic vinaigrette

serves 4 friends | as a main

This is a laid back, casual recipe for a night with friends, just hanging out. I love chicken, and I love a roasted bird with stuffing. What I don't like is all the stuffing inside that usually just stays mushy, so this is what I call my "Un-Stuffed Chicken with Texture." It's my way of making a crispy bird with crispy stuffing that has something going on between your teeth! Chew on that one!

[for the chicken]
4 cups water
½ cup kosher salt
2 small birds (poussins, medium roasters), cut in half
Kosher salt and freshly ground black pepper, to taste
¼ stick (1 ounce) butter

[for the oven-dried tomatoes]
12 cherry tomatoes, halved
Olive oil, to coat
Kosher salt and freshly ground black pepper, to taste
1 tablespoon fresh garlic, minced
1 sprig thyme, leaves only

[for the garlic confit]
¼ cup canola or olive oil
½ cup whole fresh garlic cloves, peeled

[for the bread salad]
¼ stick (1 ounce) butter
1 tablespoon extra virgin olive oil
½ cup Kalamata olives, pitted and halved
2 cups croutons, crushed
¼ cup basil, sliced into thin strips
1 lemon, zested and juiced

[for the vinaigrette]
¼ cup balsamic vinegar
2 tablespoons extra virgin olive oil

[how to do it]

Chef's note: This chicken needs to be brined a minimum of 6 hours or overnight.

1. Prepare the chicken: In a medium pot, bring the water with the salt to a boil, stirring to dissolve. Remove from heat and cool in refrigerator. Place the chickens in a container big enough to hold them, but small enough so they will be completely submerged in the salt water when you pour it in. Cover and refrigerate for 6 hours or overnight.
2. Preheat oven to 150°F.
3. Make the oven-dried tomatoes: In a small bowl, combine all the ingredients and toss to coat the tomatoes well. Lay them out on a sheet pan and bake for 3 hours.
4. Make the garlic confit: In a small saucepot on medium-high, heat the oil and the garlic and cook until the garlic starts to caramelize. Remove from heat and set aside.
5. Cook the chicken: Raise oven temperature to 350°F. Remove the chicken from the brine, rinse in cold water, and pat dry. Season all over with salt and pepper. Place the chickens on a large sheet pan or roasting pan skin side up and cook for 30 minutes. Reset oven to broil. Broil for about 10 to 15 minutes, so the skin gets nice and crispy, rubbing periodically with butter to moisten.
6. Make the bread salad: In a medium sauté pan, heat the butter and olive oil and add 1 cup of the oven-dried tomatoes, ¼ cup garlic confit, the olives, and croutons. Toss together and add the basil, zest and juice. Stir well to combine and keep warm.
7. Make the vinaigrette: In a small bowl, combine the vinegar and oil with a quick whisk (not very much). Pour over the cooked chicken, being sure to coat all of the meat.
8. To serve: Go family-style on this one. Put the chicken out on a big ol' platter and serve up the bread salad in a big ol' bowl!

GABARDINE

COME SCRIBE!

WINEMAKER

big mac n cheese + caramelized onions + white cheddar fondue

serves 4 friends | as a main

All right, the first thing to do when you do a mac and cheese is make it your own. Use the things you like best — use any pasta you want and toss in just about any delicious thing you love — shrimp, pulled pork, salami, whatever makes you feel warm and fuzzy. I say load it up! Make that big mac and cheese even bigger, until it's a Humongous Mac ready to rip up the town!

[for the oven-dried tomatoes]
12 cherry tomatoes, halved
Olive oil, to coat
Kosher salt and freshly ground black pepper, to taste
1 tablespoon fresh garlic, minced
1 sprig thyme, leaves only

[for the garlic confit]
¼ cup canola or olive oil
½ cup whole fresh garlic cloves, peeled

[for the pasta]
1 pound fusilli (or your favorite pasta)

[for the fondue]
2 cups heavy cream
1 cup white cheddar, shredded
1 cup mozzarella, shredded
¼ cup freshly grated Parmesan cheese
¼ stick (1 ounce) butter
¼ cup all-purpose flour
⅓ cup Kalamata olives, pitted

[finishing touches]
1 tablespoon Italian parsley, minced
½ cup panko bread crumbs
Extra virgin olive oil

[how to do it]

1. Preheat oven to 150°F.
2. Make the oven-dried tomatoes: In a small bowl, combine all the ingredients and toss to coat the tomatoes well. Lay them out face up on a sheet pan and cook in the oven for 3 hours.
3. Make the garlic confit: In a small saucepan on medium-high, heat the oil and the garlic and cook until the garlic starts to caramelize. Remove from heat and set aside.
4. Cook the pasta: Put a large pot of water on the stove to boil and cook your pasta *al dente*, so it's nearly done but not quite. Drain and set aside.
5. Make the fondue: In a medium saucepan, bring the cream to a boil and stir in the cheeses to melt and combine. In a small saucepan, melt the butter and get it hot. Whisk in the flour to create a roux (a buttery paste). Continue whisking until it thickens up and all the clumps are gone.
6. Ladle some of the hot cream into the roux and whisk to combine thoroughly (this will loosen up the roux and make it easier to incorporate). Gradually add the roux mix into the heavy cream, whisking constantly to combine and smooth. Cook the mixture until it thickens, but not too thick (it will thicken more as it cools).
7. Raise oven temperature to 350°F.
8. Assemble the mac n cheese: In a large sauté pan on medium heat, pour in about half of the fondue mixture and add the pasta. Cook and stir to coat the pasta (as it cooks it will absorb the cheesy fondue). Add more cheese mixture to the pasta to coat thoroughly.
9. Mix in the oven-dried tomatoes, olives, and 3 to 4 cloves of confit garlic and stir to combine. Transfer the pasta to an oven-proof baking dish (or 4 individual baking dishes, if you have them) and top off with the remaining fondue (the mixture should be wet and creamy).
10. Top the pasta with the parsley and bread crumbs, and drizzle olive oil generously on top. Bake in the oven until the top is crispy and dark brown and the cheese is hot and bubbly, about 10 to 15 minutes. You're ready to roll!

abalone + uni benedict + brown butter hollandaise

serves 4 friends | as a main

I'm so lucky to live in a place (and to have restaurants in a place) where you can literally see the water where my uni (sea urchin) is collected. If I time it right, I can have uni sitting on your plate within 30 minutes of pulling it from the Pacific. (To my fans in the Midwest: my apologies. You can get uni by mail order.) I created this as a brunch item, partly to celebrate fresh San Diego seafood, partly because uni is one of my most-favorite things, but mostly because it's so freakin' cool to cook with these ingredients, I have to do it! So ... if you can get it ... go for it!

[for the hollandaise]
1 stick (4 ounces) butter
2 egg yolks
¼ cup hot water, plus extra if needed
Half lemon, for squeezing
Tabasco sauce, to taste
Kosher salt and freshly ground black pepper, to taste
2 uni, split in half, exposing lobes (the orange clump of caviar-like deliciousness)
1 teaspoon fresh chives, minced

[for the eggs]
1 tablespoon white vinegar
Pinch or two kosher salt
4 eggs

[for the abalone]
1 tablespoon butter
1 tablespoon canola oil
2 (8-ounce) abalone steaks (get the ones that are pre-tenderized or ask your fishmonger), each cut in half
1 cup all-purpose flour, on a plate
2 eggs, whisked, on a plate
1 cup panko bread crumbs, on a plate
Kosher salt and freshly ground black pepper, to taste
Half lemon, for squeezing

[finishing touches]
4 slices buttered and grilled focaccia, Italian bread, or other crusty bread

[how to do it]

1. Make the hollandaise: In a sauté pan on high, melt the butter and bring it to a hard boil (it will foam up at first, then the foam will die down and the milk solids will start to cook). When the butter turns a golden brown, take it off the heat and let it cool slightly.
2. In a blender, combine the yolks with ¼ cup hot water on medium-high speed for about 20 seconds. Slowly start ladling in the brown butter, in a slow, steady stream. If the mixture gets too thick, add a few drops of water. When all the butter has incorporated, squeeze in a little lemon juice, a couple of drops of Tabasco, and salt and pepper.
3. Gently whisk in 2 lobes of the uni (reserve the other 2 lobes for the garnish). Mix in the chives. Keep the hollandaise warm, but not hot, until needed.
4. Pre-poach the eggs: In a small pot, bring a few cups of water with the vinegar and salt to a gentle simmer (not a rolling boil!). Gently slide the eggs into the water and cook until the whites become solid. With a slotted spoon, gently lift the eggs out, and place them in a bowl of ice water to stop the cooking. Save the hot water in the pot.
5. Cook the abalone: In a large sauté pan, heat the butter and oil to hot. Dip the abalone pieces first in the flour, then in the egg, then in the bread crumbs and place them in the hot pan. Sear them until they are a dark, golden brown on both sides. Season with salt and pepper, and finish with a squeeze of lemon.
6. Reheat the water in the pot and gently slide the eggs back in to reheat, about 30 seconds.
7. To serve: Place the abalone on the bread and the egg on top. Adorn the egg with a generous dollop of hollandaise and top that off with half a lobe of uni, set atop this delicious creation.

cook's toast + blackberry port syrup + a side of guilt

serves 4 friends | as a main

Funny story: We didn't have French toast at Gabardine when we first opened. And so, during our very first brunch, the second person that walks into the restaurant says, "I want to have some French toast." Well, I never say no to a guest – and I'm always up for a good challenge — so we cracked up a bunch of eggs, threw in some milk and vanilla, and whipped together our quick French toast (also known as French toast à la minute!). And here's the kicker: the guy who requested it? His last name was Cook. How perfect is that? I told him I'd name the dish after him, since he made me make it — so now we have Cook's Toast!

[for the syrup]
1 pint fresh blackberries
1 cup port
¼ cup granulated sugar

[for the topping aka side of guilt]
1½ cups cream cheese
½ cup butter, at room temperature
1 cup powdered sugar

[for the toast]
½ stick (2 ounces) butter
6 eggs
⅓ cup milk
3 to 4 drops pure vanilla extract
4 large, thick pieces of focaccia or French/Italian loaf (these pieces need to be big, honkin' obnoxious, long slices of bread!)

[finishing touches]
Fresh strawberries

[how to do it]

1. Make the syrup: In a small saucepot over medium heat, add half the blackberries, the port, and the sugar. Stir well to dissolve the sugar and let it cook down to a nice, syrupy consistency. Strain and allow to cool down. Gently fold in the remaining blackberries and set aside until needed.
2. Make the topping: Combine the ingredients in a mixing bowl or stand mixer. Beat on medium speed until smooth, creamy, and airy. Chill until needed.
3. Make the toast: In a large sauté pan, melt the butter on high and let it froth up. After the foam dies down, let the milk solids cook until the butter turns a nice golden brown. Remove from heat and pour into a cup or something you can dispense from (you can leave enough in the pan to cook the first side of the toast).
4. In a medium bowl, combine the eggs, milk, and vanilla and whisk together well to incorporate. Soak the bread in the mixture, turning to coat and soak both sides. Put the bread in the hot sauté pan and cook until browned on one side. Flip and cook to brown on the second side.
5. To serve: Place a piece of toast on each plate, drizzle a generous amount of syrup over each, and top each with a honkin' dollop of topping. Garnish with more fresh berries, if desired. Grab the Champagne and let's have some brunch!

gbone

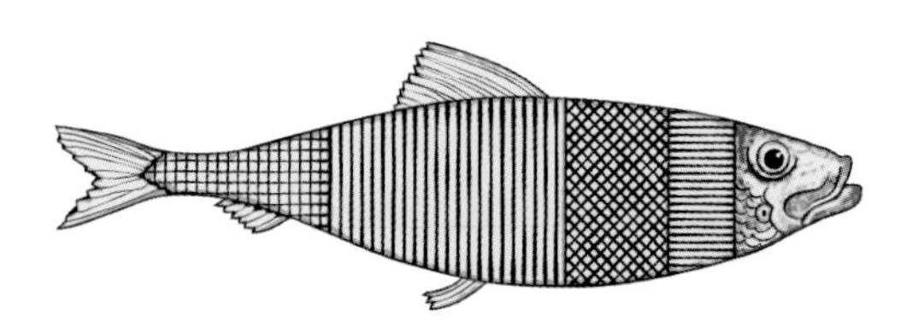

Herringbone

LA JOLLA, CALIFORNIA

Fish Meats Field

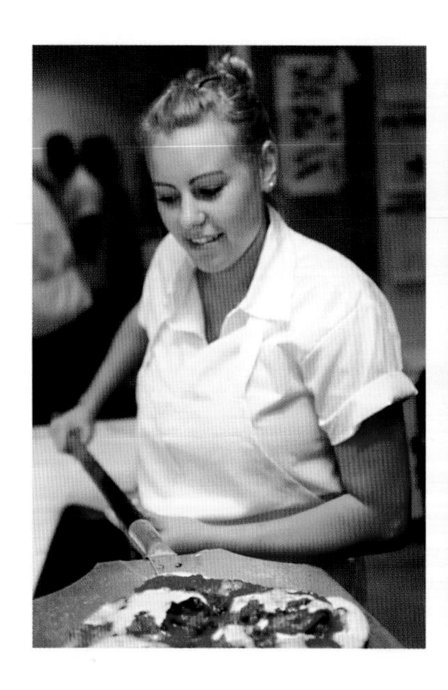

HERRINGBONE, IN MY MIND, IS THE "SOPHISTICATED LADY" OF THE GROUP; KIND OF THE "chardonnay" in our wine cellar. Set in a gorgeous old brick building in La Jolla, this restaurant is all about classic American seafood dishes and showing off the freshest ingredients we can find from the sea and land together. Thomas Schoos nailed the design — it's the most beautiful thing in the world. With 100-year-old olive trees growing right inside the space, the huge, glass-walled display kitchen, the wood-burning pizza oven, it's a virtual masterpiece. After doing four other restaurants, I would say Herringbone is the one where we absolutely killed it — we got everything right; the right space, the right chef, the right combination of flavors and ingredients on the menu. We wanted to take the root words — the *herring* and the *bone* — and use those as our inspiration for really fun combinations (like our clam and bone marrow pizza). We played with all kinds of surf and turf combinations, and wound up with a fresh, engaging, unstuffy menu that appeals to people who know and love great seafood and like it done with a healthy respect for tradition (but not so healthy that it's boring!). We like to refer to Herringbone as "fish meats field," where the best of the land comes together with the best from the sea.

Chef Amanda Baumgarten

It's been very exciting to be able to work with Amanda Baumgarten, a fellow "Top Chef" alum (season 7) and an all-around great chef. From the very start, she's taken my basic concepts and ideas, has developed them, and has evolved them and shot them into the stratosphere. Amanda brings a real passion for the farm-to-table concept to her kitchen: she picks up her own Northwest and East Coast fish from the airport, and she often travels to farms around the county to pick up the freshest produce available. Amanda has really opened my eyes to the beauty and flavor of really fresh, well-prepared greens, radishes, tomatoes, and other vegetables. The enthusiasm and energy that she brings to Herringbone are unparalleled. I truly admire her finesse as a chef. Whereas I like to wield a fairly heavy hand — I like to season big; I like to brown, caramelize, and char things — Amanda has a much lighter touch, with more subtlety and grace. It's just what you'd expect from the "sophisticated lady" in the social dining group.

smoked trout dip

serves 4 friends | as an app

When we were first planning Herringbone, I told Chef Amanda that I wanted a smoked mahi, but her eyes didn't exactly light up at that request. So she did a little research and came back with her own great idea, which was inspired by hot smoked trout dip — a classic dish from Wisconsin using lake trout and Wisconsin "brick" cheese, which is a mild cheddar. What you get is smoky, creamy, rich, delicious flavors that are great warm or cold. Slather up a thick piece of grilled sourdough and chomp away!

[for the dip]

- ¼ cup olive oil
- ¼ cup yellow onion, finely chopped
- 2 cloves fresh garlic, minced
- 1 pound smoked trout, skinned, boned, and flaked into pieces
- 1 cup sour cream
- 1 cup mayonnaise
- 1 lemon, zested and juiced
- ½ cup finely grated Parmesan cheese
- 1 cup finely grated brick white cheddar
- 3 tablespoons fresh chives, finely minced
- ⅛ teaspoon ground white pepper
- ¼ teaspoon kosher salt

[finishing touches]

- Crusty sourdough bread, sliced
- Olive oil
- Fresh chives, finely minced

[how to do it]

Chef's note: A good online source for smoked trout is Browne Trading, www.brownetrading.com.

1. Preheat oven to 350°F.
2. **Make the dip:** In a large sauté pan, heat the oil to hot on medium heat. Add the onions and garlic and sweat them (covered) until they are translucent. Set aside to cool.
3. In a large bowl, crumble the trout with your fingers into smaller pieces (but not to small — I love good texture, so you don't need to make it super fine). Add the remaining ingredients and mix well to combine. Season with white pepper and salt to taste.
4. Transfer the dip to an ovenproof baking dish and pop it in the oven for 10 minutes, or until it is nice and melty and molten.
5. While the dip is baking, brush the bread with olive oil and grill it or throw it under the broiler for a minute. Cut your bread into nice size dipping pieces, put the dip in the center of your coffee table or patio table, and go to town!

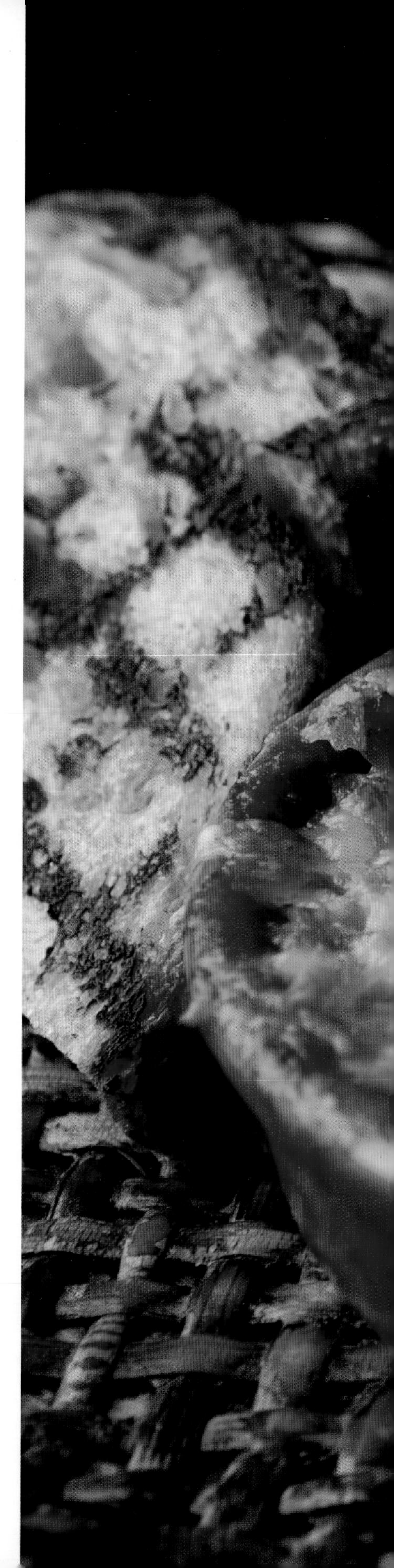

baked clams + smoky bacon crust

serves 2 friends as a main | serves 4 friends as an app

Chef Amanda is a bit of an "East-Coast groupie" when it comes to iconic seafood dishes, and she loves doing her own takes on regional American classics like baked clams: It doesn't get more classic than that. Super simple. The crust for this recipe is an aromatic herbal mix, with lemon, butter, and one of Amanda's favorite secret ingredients: Ritz crackers. Yup! You got it! Another American classic! Straight out of the box and into the crust. Hey, if it tastes good, use it!

[for the crust]

4 sticks (1 pound) butter, softened, divided use
¼ pound smoked bacon, minced
¼ cup yellow onion, minced
3 cloves fresh garlic, minced
1 cup white wine
1 cup fresh parsley, roughly chopped
1 cup fresh chives, roughly chopped
½ cup fresh oregano, chopped
1 lemon, zested and juiced
2 cups Ritz crackers, crushed
Kosher salt and freshly ground black pepper, to taste

[finishing touches]

24 cherrystone clams, shucked
4 to 8 lemon wedges

[how to do it]

1. Preheat oven broiler.
2. Start the crust: Heat a large sauté pan on medium-high heat with 1 tablespoon of butter. When the butter is melted, add the bacon and sauté until slightly golden. Add the onion and garlic and cook until they become translucent, about 5 to 7 minutes.
3. Add the wine and reduce until there is virtually no liquid left in the pan. Set aside to cool.
4. In a food processor, process the chopped herbs and the remainder of the softened butter until well blended. Add the bacon mixture, lemon juice, zest, and cracker crumbs, and process until you have a bright green, smooth, buttery crust mixture. Season with salt and pepper to taste.
5. Remove the crust mix from the food processor and let it hang out at room temperature while you shuck your clams (so it'll be easy to spread).
6. Prepare the clams: Take a spoon and smooth the crust over the top of each clam. (Try not to lose the juice in the clams – it's SUPER tasty!) Put the clams in an ovenproof dish (you can put some rock salt in the bottom of the dish to keep them from tipping over, which will help the crust brown evenly) and broil until the crust is nice and golden brown. Transfer to a serving platter with plenty of lemon wedges and a great bottle of white wine.

[**Chef Amanda's Tip: "Shucking clams can be a bit tricky. I'm gonna do my best to describe it to you, but if you haven't done it before, I'd suggest YouTube-ing it as well. In order to shuck clams, you need a clam knife (go figure). You can pick one of these up at a Williams-Sonoma or pretty much any cooking store near you for a few bucks. Grab a dish towel and nestle the clam with the side that opens facing out in the towel. With your other hand, grab the knife. Be careful! There is a small space where the two sides of the shell meet that you want to slide the knife into. Gently work the knife back and forth and pry the clam open. Try not to get frustrated — the end result is well worth it. Once all of your clams are open, you should have some nice clams on the half shell!"**]

bitter greens + anchovies + thyme croutons

serves 8 friends | as an app

The garlicky-lemony dressing in this salad is the perfect match for the escarole, endive, dandelion greens, and Treviso we mix together. When you add the saltiness of capers and the anchovy, you've got an awesome riff on the classic Caesar, but it's not a Caesar! It's even bitter (I mean better)! This is a rustic salad, chunky and full of big flavors. You eat this salad with a knife and fork!

[for the croutons]
1 loaf rustic sourdough bread, torn into 1-inch pieces
½ cup extra virgin olive oil
1 tablespoon fresh garlic, minced
6 sprigs fresh thyme
1 lemon, zested

[for the greens]
2 heads curly endive
2 heads Treviso (or radicchio)
2 heads escarole
1 bunch dandelion greens

[for the dressing]
8 cloves fresh garlic
2 anchovies, cleaned
1 tablespoon capers, drained
1 tablespoon whole grain mustard
2 egg yolks
2 tablespoons freshly squeezed lemon juice
2 tablespoons red wine vinegar
1½ cups extra virgin olive oil
½ bunch fresh Italian parsley, finely chopped
Kosher salt and freshly ground black pepper, to taste

[finishing touches]
Freshly shaved Pecorino cheese
Anchovies

[how to do it]

1. Preheat oven to 350°F.
2. Make the croutons: In a large bowl, combine the bread chunks with the other ingredients until the bread is well coated. Transfer to a sheet tray and bake for 7 to 10 minutes, making sure to rotate the tray halfway through the cooking time. The croutons are done when they're nice and golden brown. Allow them to cool to room temperature.
3. Prepare the greens: Break down all the lettuces into leaves. Fill a sink with cold water and wash the lettuce very well. Remove the leaves from the water and use a salad spinner to dry. (I like my salads to require a fork and knife so I leave the lettuce pieces quite big: however, feel free to cut them down).
4. Make the dressing: In a blender, combine all the ingredients (except the oil and parsley) on medium speed until well blended. Drizzle in the olive oil in a slow, steady stream until well incorporated (the dressing should be nice and creamy!).
5. Transfer the dressing to a jar or storage container, add the chopped parsley, and season to taste with kosher salt and black pepper. Use immediately or store in the fridge for up to 1 week.
6. Assemble and serve the salad: In a large bowl, toss the lettuce with some dressing, shaved Pecorino cheese, and the croutons. Taste and add more dressing or seasoning if necessary. Transfer to a serving platter and garnish with anchovies.

"I'm all about delivering to our guests. That means creating dishes that are interesting, super tasty, and also deliver the flavors people want when they order. If you order clam chowder, you want clam chowder. You don't want anyone to get all cheffy and weird with it."

— Chef Amanda

clam chowder

serves 8 to 10 friends | as an app

Here's another American seafood classic: New England-style clam chowder. No clams out of a can for this one — you need a pile of big, juicy, fresh clams in the shell for this. This is also a chowder that requires two hands: pull out those clams and don't forget a big hunk of crusty delicious bread for each person. Soaking up the buttery, creamy sauce with the bread is one of the best parts of chowing this chowder!

[for the chowder base]
¼ cup canola or vegetable oil
½ pound smoked bacon, diced small
2 pounds yellow onion, diced small
1 pound carrots, diced small
1 pound celery, diced small
8 cups heavy cream
6 cups clam juice
1 stick (4 ounces) unsalted butter
1 cup all-purpose flour
Kosher salt and ground white pepper, to taste

[for the clams]
1 pound fresh Manila clams (or cockles or sunbursts)
2 cups white wine
4 springs fresh thyme
2 cloves fresh garlic, smashed

[finishing touches]
Great, crusty sourdough bread
Fresh chives, finely minced

[how to do it]

1. **Start the chowder base:** Heat a large stockpot with the oil until it just starts to smoke. Throw in the diced bacon and render it until it's nice and crispy. Strain the bacon (I love to save the bacon fat and spread it on toast!).
2. In the same pot on medium-high heat, add the onions, carrots, and celery (the pot will have some color left from when you rendered the bacon. Don't wash it out!! That's the base of your flavor in the chowder). Sweat the veggies (covered) until the onions are translucent.
3. Add the cream and clam juice and bring to a simmer. Ladle out 4 cups of liquid from the soup.
4. In a sauté pan, melt the butter and whisk the flour into it until it forms a smooth paste (this is called a roux — it thickens the chowder).
5. Add the 4 cups of liquid you took from the soup to the roux and bring it to a boil. This mixture should be quite thick. Once it boils, pour it back into the pot with the soup, and simmer for 10 minutes. Taste and adjust the seasoning with the kosher salt and ground white pepper to taste. Remove the pot from the heat.
6. **Now for the clams:** Rinse them under cold running water for about 10 minutes (this helps get the sand out). Place them in a bowl with the wine, thyme, and garlic.
7. Get another large sauté pan (with a lid) and get it smoking hot. Dump the clams and all their goodies right into the hot pan and cover immediately. (This part should be kind of exciting. It'll make a lot of steam, a rad sizzling noise, and be very dramatic.) Shake the pan back and forth a few times. The clams are cooked when they all open up (this should take about 90 seconds).
8. **To serve:** Remove the clams from the sauté pan as soon as they open and discard any clams that do not open after 2 to 3 minutes. Now, you're ready to serve! Throw the steamed clams (shell and all) into a large soup terrine, pour the chowder on top, garnish with chives, pull some bowls from the cupboard, and serve it up with some sourdough and a great bottle (or two) of sauvignon blanc!

crab cakes + grain mustard rémoulade + homemade garlic pickles

serves 4 friends | as a main

If you're going to have a crab cake recipe on the menu at one of my restaurants, it better be awesome, 'cause we don't do "ordinary!" I love this one because it has a great mix of flavors and textures going on in it. It's got the crunchy, it's got the lemon, it's got the mustard, and when you fry it all up, you've got a kick-ass crab cake. Top it with a heaping pile of our spicy rémoulade for the final zing, and you got it goin' on!

[for the pickles]

1 white or yellow onion, cut into ¼-inch slices
6 cloves fresh garlic, roughly chopped
3 cups water
1 tablespoon kosher salt
3 cups white wine vinegar
10 Kirby cucumbers (or similar), rinsed and halved lengthwise
1 nice big handful fresh dill

[for the crab cakes]

1 whole egg
¼ cup heavy cream
½ Granny Smith apple (or similar), peeled, finely chopped
1 teaspoon fresh chives, finely chopped
1 stalk celery, finely chopped
1 clove fresh garlic, minced
¼ cup yellow onion, finely chopped
2 tablespoons butter
2 lemons, zested and juiced
1 tablespoon Worcestershire sauce
1 tablespoon Tabasco sauce
2 tablespoons mayonnaise
2 tablespoons Dijon mustard
1 tablespoon Old Bay seasoning (I love this stuff!)
2 tablespoons fresh parsley, finely chopped
2 pounds jumbo lump crab, picked clean
2 cups Ritz crackers, crumbled
2 cups panko bread crumbs
¼ cup oil or clarified butter, for frying

[for the rémoulade]

¼ cup buttermilk
1 cup mayonnaise
1 tablespoon whole grain mustard
1 lemon, juiced
1 tablespoon capers, finely chopped
1 tablespoon shallot, finely chopped
2 tablespoons celery root, grated
1 teaspoon Tabasco sauce
¼ teaspoon cayenne powder
Kosher salt and freshly ground black pepper, to taste
1 tablespoon fresh parsley, finely chopped

[finishing touch]

Pickled red onions

[how to do it]

Chef's note: For homemade pickles, start this recipe at least a day ahead. Now, you don't need to serve this crab cake with pickles, but I'd recommend it. Pickles are super easy. The downside is they require advance planning on your part. It's up to you. Homemade pickles are always a nice thing to have hanging out in the fridge, though, so keep that in mind.

1. Prepare the pickles: In a large stockpot, combine the onion, garlic, water, salt, and vinegar and bring to a boil. In the meantime, put the cucumbers in a container (glass is best) with the handful of dill. Once the pickling liquid boils, pour it over the cucumbers (completely submerge them) and let them sit outside the fridge until they drop to room temperature. (It's helpful to put a plate on top to weigh them down, so they all pickle evenly.) Once they are cool, put them in the fridge for a minimum of a day. (They'll only get better with every day after that!) They'll hang out in the fridge very nicely for a month.

2. Prepare the crab cake mixture: In a large bowl, mix all the ingredients together (except the crab, the crackers, and the panko) and combine well. Add the crab and combine gently to incorporate.

3. In a food processor, pulse the Ritz crackers and the bread crumbs until they have the consistency of graham cracker crumbs. Reserve 2 cups for coating the crab cakes before cooking.
4. Incorporate the bread-crumb mixture into the crab. When you do this, be careful not to break up the lump crabmeat too much. (You really want to have that texture in the cakes.) Now you're ready to mold your cakes. Use a 2- to 3-inch diameter cookie cutter or ring mold that is about 2 inches tall. Fill the molds with the crab mix and pack them nice and tight. The tighter you pack, the better your cakes will hold up when you cook them. Store all of your molded cakes on a sheet tray in the fridge until you're ready to cook them.
5. **Make the rémoulade:** In a medium bowl, combine all the ingredients (except the salt, pepper, and parsley) and mix well. Season with salt and pepper and finish with the parsley. Taste and adjust seasoning if necessary. Refrigerate until ready to serve.
6. Preheat oven to 375°F.
7. **Cook the crab cakes:** Heat a large nonstick pan on high heat and add ¼ cup of clarified butter or cooking oil. Remove the crab cakes from the fridge and coat them in the 2 cups of the cracker mixture. Sear them in the pan until they're golden brown on one side, then flip them over and pop them into the oven (in the pan) for about 6 minutes. (Keeping them in the pan while they're in the oven enables the bottoms to get nice and brown while they heat through.) Test for doneness by poking them with a cake tester or metal skewer and testing the temperature on the inside of your wrist. If it's hot, you're good to go!
8. Arrange each cake on a plate with some sliced pickles and a dollop of rémoulade and dig in!

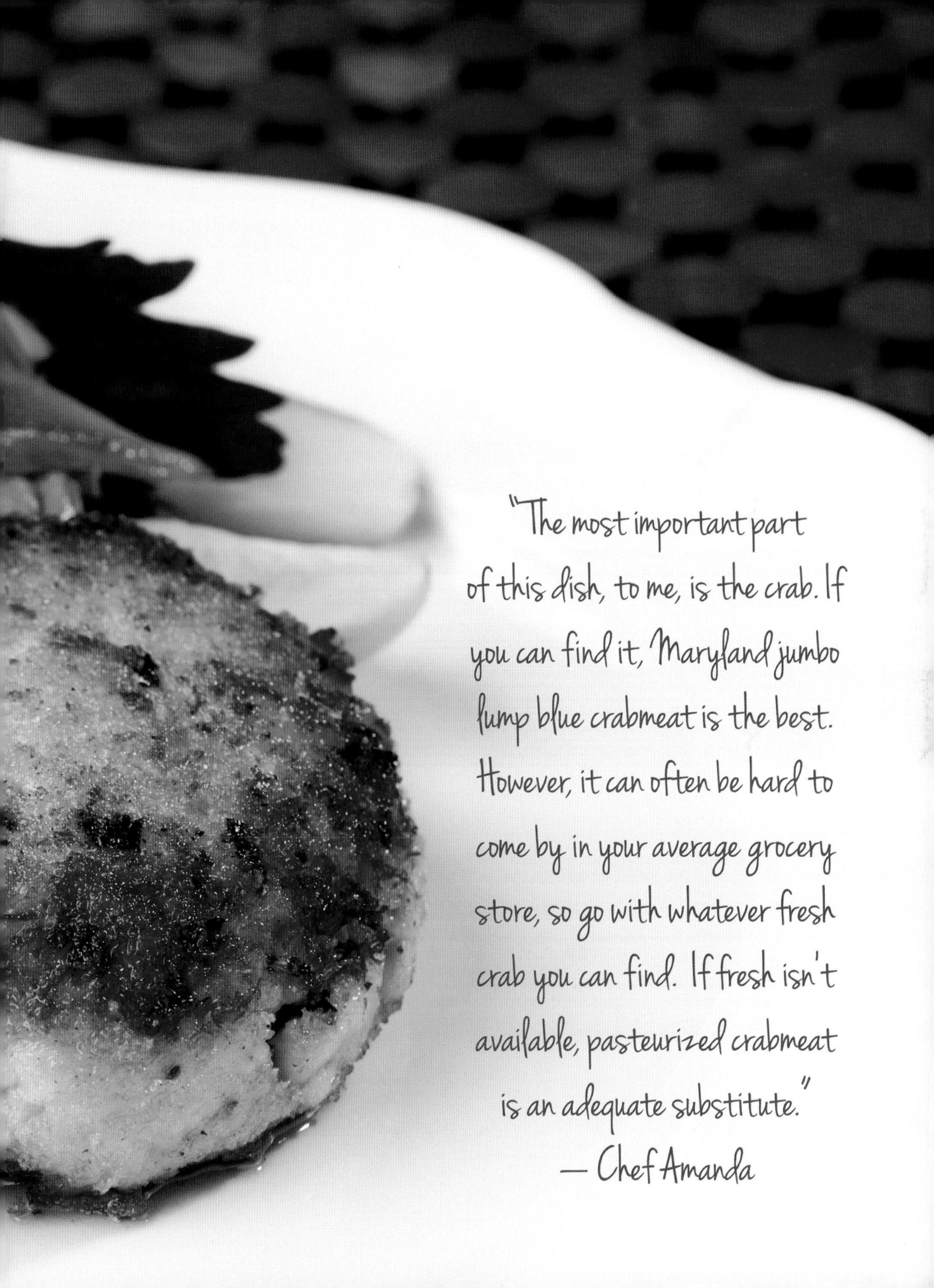
"The most important part of this dish, to me, is the crab. If you can find it, Maryland jumbo lump blue crabmeat is the best. However, it can often be hard to come by in your average grocery store, so go with whatever fresh crab you can find. If fresh isn't available, pasteurized crabmeat is an adequate substitute."
— Chef Amanda

whole fish + roasted fennel + wild rice + tomato caper sauce

serves 2 friends | as a main

I was so stoked to get a wood-burning oven for Herringbone! There are so many things you can cook in it, and everything you take out of it tastes great! Chef Amanda does her whole fish in the wood-burning oven, with a blend of oak and olive wood, and she keeps the preparation super simple. With a great fresh fish and some lemon, garlic, oil, and oregano, that's all you need. Of course, if you're not lucky enough to have a wood-burning oven, you can do this really easily in an oven or on a grill. When it's done, put it on the biggest platter you can find, garnish it up, and show it off! Present it to your guests with fanfare — trumpets playing in the background!

[for the rice]
2 to 3 tablespoons butter, divided use
1 shallot, minced
2 cups wild rice
1 teaspoon kosher salt
Freshly ground black pepper, to taste
2 sprigs fresh thyme
6 cups water

[for the roasted fennel]
3 tablespoons olive oil
3 heads fennel, washed and quartered
1 pinch kosher salt
Freshly ground black pepper, to taste
3 sprigs fresh thyme

[for the fish]
2-pound snapper, gutted and scaled
Kosher salt and freshly ground black pepper, to taste
4 (⅛-inch) lemon slices
1 clove fresh garlic, smashed
2 sprigs fresh oregano
1 tablespoon olive oil

[for the tomato sauce]
1 cup extra virgin olive oil, divided use
2 shallots, minced
3 cloves fresh garlic, minced
¼ cup capers
¼ cup cherry tomatoes, halved
2 lemons, juiced
2 tablespoons fresh parsley, chopped

[finishing touches]
Lemon slices
Orange sections
Toasted pine nuts
Arugula

[how to do it]

Chef's note: When you purchase your fish, ask your fishmonger to scale it and remove the gills and guts. It'll save you from making a big mess at home.

1. **Make the rice:** Heat the butter in a medium stockpot on medium heat. When the butter is melted, cook the shallots with a pinch of salt until they're nice and translucent. Add the rice and cook for a few minutes to coat well with the butter and shallot mixture. Season again with salt and pepper.
2. Add the thyme sprigs and water, and bring the mixture to a boil, stirring constantly. Reduce the heat to low, cover, and simmer until the rice is cooked, about 40 minutes. Add another tablespoon of butter and check your seasoning again before serving.
3. Preheat oven to 350°F.
4. **Make the fennel:** Heat the olive oil in a large sauté pan on high heat. Season the fennel with salt and pepper and sear the cut sides in the pan until they're golden brown. Transfer the fennel to a roasting dish,

spread the thyme over the top, cover with foil, and roast in the oven until tender, about 30 minutes.
5. Increase oven to 375°F.
6. Prepare the fish: This recipe calls for a 2-pound snapper, but any fish of a similar size will work. Season the fish inside and out with salt and pepper. Stuff the cavity with the lemon slices, garlic, and oregano.
7. Grease a large piece of parchment paper with the olive oil. Lay the fish down on the paper and roll the paper up around the fish. Tie both ends with some butcher's twine and pop it into the oven for 15 to 20 minutes. (You can test the doneness by sticking a cake tester into the parcel. If it is hot to the touch, your fish is done!)
8. Make the tomato sauce: Heat a medium saucepot on medium heat with 2 tablespoons of olive oil. Cook the shallots and garlic until they are nice and soft. Add the capers and cherry tomatoes and heat through only lightly, for about 1 minute. (You don't want to really cook the tomatoes, you only want to release a touch of their flavor into the pan.) Remove the pot from the heat and add the lemon juice and the remainder of your olive oil. Taste and season with salt and pepper. Finish with chopped parsley.
9. To serve: Transfer the cooked fish to a large serving platter. Unwrap the parchment and garnish the platter with the roasted fennel. Serve the rice and the tomato caper sauce on the side and tell your guests to dig in!

"When you can
get great, fresh fish, the best
strategy is often to cook it quickly and simply.
You can do this recipe with whatever fish you like —
just keep the ingredients simple and let the
flavor of the fish take center stage."
— Chef Amanda

swordfish caponata + pickled raisins + tomato fondue

serves 8 friends | as a main

I love pickling! That's why all my restaurants have a bunch of different kinds of pickles on the menu, as well as pickled things in the dishes themselves. Here, Chef Amanda throws pickled raisins into a classic Italian swordfish preparation (you can do it with albacore, too) and has put a few other little fresh spins in there as well. Sweet, sour, salty — it's all in here! And it screams pinot grigio!

[for the pickled raisins]
2 teaspoons mustard seeds
1 cup white wine vinegar
½ cup water
1 sprig fresh thyme
1 sprig fresh rosemary
1 arbol chile
½ cup granulated sugar
½ pound golden raisins
1 teaspoon kosher salt

[for the tomato fondue]
¼ cup olive oil
½ yellow onion, diced small
1 tablespoon fresh garlic, minced
2 tablespoons tomato paste
2 pounds Roma tomatoes, blanched, peeled, seeded (See tip, opposite page)
4 sprigs fresh thyme
Kosher salt and freshly ground black pepper, to taste

[for the caponata]
1 cup olive oil, divided use
2 large eggplants, diced
1 teaspoon cumin seed
1 teaspoon ground cinnamon
½ teaspoon ground clove
1 tablespoon cocoa powder
2 red bell peppers, thinly sliced
2 yellow bell peppers, thinly sliced
1 yellow onion, thinly sliced
1 tablespoon fresh garlic, minced
1 arbol chile
3 sprigs fresh thyme
1 bay leaf
1 cup red wine
¼ cup balsamic vinegar
¼ cup capers, drained
¼ cup pine nuts, toasted
2 tablespoons dark brown sugar
Kosher salt and freshly ground black pepper, to taste

[for the swordfish]
8 (8-ounce, 1-inch thick) fresh swordfish filets
Kosher salt and freshly ground black pepper, to taste
Oil olive
8 sprigs fresh rosemary

[finishing touch]
Extra virgin olive oil

[**Chef Amanda's Tip: Blanching tomatoes before peeling them makes it really easy to get the skins off and the seeds out. Get a pot of boiling water (should be big enough to submerge the tomatoes) and some ice water at the ready. Take a small knife and make an "x" in the bottom of each tomato. Be careful not to cut too far into the tomato, just into the skin. Dunk your tomatoes in the boiling water for 10 to 15 seconds and immediately drop them in your ice water. Depending on the size of your pot, you might want to do this in batches so that the water temperature doesn't drop (this makes for mushy tomatoes). Take a small knife and peel off the skin and discard. Cut the tomatoes in half and use a spoon to scoop out the seeds and discard.**]

[how to do it]

Chef's note: For this particular recipe, I recommend grilling the fish if you have the means. If not, sautéing will work just as well. So, if you have a grill, fire it up! Grilling fish can be a little tricky. You want to have one side of your grill hot and one side kind of on the medium to low side. Basically, you need to start the fish on the hot side to keep it from sticking. Also, pull your fish out of the fridge about half an hour before you plan on grilling it.

1. Make the pickled raisins: In a dry, medium saucepot, toast the mustard seeds on medium heat. Add the remaining ingredients, liquids first, and simmer until the liquid becomes syrupy and the raisins are nice and plump, about 10 minutes. Remove from the heat and set aside.
2. Make the tomato fondue: Heat a large sauté pan on medium heat, add ¼ cup of olive oil and get it hot. Add the onions and garlic and a pinch of salt. You want to sweat the onion and garlic slow and low until they are super soft. (Make sure to turn down the heat and cover the pot while you're sweating.) Once the veggies are soft, add the tomato paste and cook until it's a nice dark red color. Add the tomatoes and thyme, season again with salt and pepper, give it a stir, and put the cover back on. (The idea here is you want to cook all of the water out of the tomatoes and concentrate their flavor.) The fondue should cook for about 20 minutes. Make sure to stir often to keep it from burning. It's done when the pan is dry and the tomatoes are soft. Remove from heat and set aside. You might have more fondue than you need for this recipe, but that's never a problem. The fondue keeps very well in the fridge (about 2 weeks) and is delicious in pasta or on toast!
3. Make the caponata: Put a large, wide pan on high heat and pour ¾ cup olive oil into the pan. (I know this sounds like a lot, but the eggplant in this dish is going to drink it up.) Once you see smoke, add the eggplant and sauté until golden brown. Remove the eggplant from the pan, drain on paper towels, and set aside.
4. Add the remaining oil to the pan and toast the cumin seed, cinnamon, clove, and cocoa powder until fragrant. Add the peppers, onions, garlic, arbol chile, thyme, and bay leaf. Make sure you sweat them thoroughly, slow and low. Once they're nice and tender, put the eggplant back in the pan and stir it up to combine and coat well.
5. Add the red wine and balsamic vinegar and reduce until most of the liquid is gone, about 85 percent of it. Fold in the capers, pine nuts, 1 cup of the pickled raisins, and ½ cup of the tomato fondue. Season with brown sugar, kosher salt, and black pepper and keep warm on low heat.
6. Preheat a grill to high or large sauté pan with 2 tablespoons of oil.
7. Cook the fish: Season the fish with salt and pepper and wipe down the grill with an oiled towel. Drop the filets on the hottest area of the grill and let them sit for 1 minute. Then rotate them a quarter turn to the left and let them sit for another minute. (This little maneuver will give you a nice criss-cross pattern on the presentation side.) Flip the fish and move the filets over to the cooler areas of the grill to finish cooking. You can brush the grilled side with a little extra virgin olive oil and place a sprig of rosemary on top of each piece. Close the grill for about 2 minutes. After 2 minutes, rotate the fish a quarter turn and close the lid again for another 2 minutes. At this point, depending on the thickness of the fish, it should be cooked.
8. Now it's time to serve: Transfer the filets to a large serving platter and put a healthy dollop of the caponata on top of each piece, drizzle the extra virgin olive oil on top, and enjoy!

seafood stew

serves 8 to 10 friends | as a main

This is another rustic dish, big and bold, and meant to share. The whole point of a seafood stew is for it to be a communal, delicious experience — and it's all about using as much fresh seafood as you can get your hands on. In the restaurant, we'll throw in some fresh Dungeness crab, some live West Coast razor clams, and fresh trimmings from our halibut and a whole bunch of other fish (all our fish comes in whole). For the broth, remember to caramelize the vegetables — that's where a lot of the base flavors are going to come from and that's where you build richness and deliciousness.

[for the seafood]
2 (1½-pound) Maine lobsters
2 (2-pound) Dungeness crabs
1 pound black mussels, rinsed and debearded
1 pound Manila clams, rinsed
1 pound shrimp (26 to 30), shelled and deveined, tails on
1 pound calamari, cleaned and cut into ¼-inch pieces
1 pound halibut, cut into 2-ounce pieces

[for the stock]
½ cup canola oil, divided use
2 lobster shells and bodies
1 pound shrimp shells
1 teaspoon cumin seed
1 teaspoon fennel seed
1 yellow onion, diced
½ pound carrots, sliced
1 head fennel, sliced
¼ cup fresh garlic, minced
1 red bell pepper, sliced
2 tablespoons tomato paste
2 cups white wine
1½ cups dry sherry
4 sprigs fresh thyme
3 sprigs fresh oregano
1 arbol chile
½ pound Roma tomatoes
4 cups (32 ounces) clam juice
8 cups (64 ounces) store-bought fish stock

[for the tomato fondue]
2 pounds Roma tomatoes, blanched, peeled, seeded (See tip, page 168)
¼ cup olive oil
½ yellow onion, diced small
1 tablespoon fresh garlic, diced small
2 tablespoons tomato paste
4 sprigs fresh thyme, leaves only

[for the rouille aka saffron and garlic mayo]
1 pinch saffron
¼ cup hot water
2 egg yolks
1 tablespoon fresh garlic, minced
1 tablespoon harissa paste (Tunisian hot chile paste; available at Whole Foods)
2 ounces freshly squeezed lemon juice
1 tablespoon Dijon mustard
2 cups extra virgin olive oil

[finishing touches]
¼ cup olive oil
½ yellow onion, minced
1 teaspoon fresh garlic, minced
½ head fennel, shaved
Small pinch red chile flakes
3 sprigs fresh thyme, leaves only
½ orange, juiced
½ lemon, juiced
Splash Pernod, optional
¼ cup fresh parsley, finely chopped

[how to do it]

Chef's note: Before beginning this recipe, check out the seafood prep tips on page 175.

1. For the seafood: Bring a large pot of salted water to a boil. First, poach the lobsters for 5 minutes and immediately submerge them in ice water. Next, poach the crabs for 14 minutes and submerge them in ice water.

"If you're having trouble locating all the seafood or don't want to use everything, don't worry about it. Seafood stew is a peasant dish that can basically include anything you want from the ocean. When it comes to seafood in this dish, the more the merrier!"

2. Once your lobsters are cool, remove the meat from the shells. Take all the cleaned and prepped fish (including the cut up halibut and calamari) and refrigerate them separately until needed.
3. **Start the stock:** Get a very large stockpot (12 quarts if you have one) nice and hot with ¼ cup of oil and throw in the lobster bodies (you want to make sure they get nice and golden brown). Add the empty lobster and shrimp shells, stirring until they turn bright red and you can smell that sweet shellfish aroma coming from the pot, about 5 minutes. Remove the shells and set aside.
4. There will be a little bit of sediment in the pot — don't wash it! This is awesome flavor! Return the pot to the heat, add another ¼ cup of oil, along with the cumin and fennel seeds. Toast these for about 30 seconds and add the onion, carrot, fennel, garlic, and bell pepper. (You want to make sure that your pot is on high heat and that you're stirring your vegetables often so that they get nice and roasted.) Once the veggies are roasted, about 5 minutes, return the shells to the pot.
5. Add the tomato paste and cook for another 90 seconds, stirring constantly (the tomato paste should turn a deep red color). Add the white wine and sherry and reduce until about a half cup of liquid remains.
6. Add the thyme, oregano, and arbol chile (if you can't find an arbol chile, any dried red chile will do). Add the Roma tomatoes, clam juice, and fish stock. Bring the stock to a boil and immediately turn it down to a simmer. It can cook for up to 1 hour.
7. **Make the tomato fondue:** Roughly chop the tomatoes. Heat ¼ cup of olive oil in a large sauté pan on medium-low heat, and cook the onions and garlic with a pinch of salt slowly until they are super soft. (Make sure to turn down the heat and cover the pot while you're cooking them.) Add the tomato paste and cook until it's a nice dark red color (just like in the stock). Add the tomatoes and thyme, season again with salt and pepper, give it a stir, and put the cover back on. (The idea here is you want to cook all of the water out of the tomatoes and concentrate their flavor.) The fondue should cook for about 20 minutes. (Make sure to stir often to keep it from burning.) It's done when the pan is dry and the tomatoes are soft. You might have more fondue than you need for this recipe, but that's never a problem. The fondue keeps up to 2 weeks in the fridge and is delicious in pasta or on toast!
8. **Prepare the rouille:** Soak the saffron in the hot water. (Saffron is very similar to tea; it'll turn the water red.)
9. Put the egg yolks, saffron "tea," garlic, harissa paste, lemon juice, and Dijon mustard in a blender on medium speed. Drizzle in the oil in a slow, steady stream. Your end result should be a creamy yellow sauce with a consistency slightly looser than mayonnaise. If you want it thicker, just use more oil.
10. Now you're ready to put the whole thing together! Strain the stock and discard the solids. Give the pot a rinse and put it back on the stove on high heat.
11. **The finishing touches:** Heat ¼ cup of olive oil in the pot and, when you see a little bit of smoke, add the minced onion, garlic, shaved fennel, and chile flakes. Give these a quick sauté and add the clams, mussels, calamari, 1 cup of tomato fondue, picked thyme, and half the stock. (You want your shellfish to open up in your stock to give it extra flavor.) Once the shellfish have opened, transfer them to a large serving bowl. Add the remainder of the stock and bring it to a simmer.
12. Add the lobster meat, crab, shrimp, and fish and let the whole mix simmer for 4 minutes. Season with salt, pepper, orange and lemon juice, and a couple drops of Pernod (if desired). Finish with parsley. When the fish is cooked and the crab and lobster are hot, pour the soup into the serving bowl with the clams and mussels and drizzle the rouille over the top. Then pat yourself on the back and ring the dinner bell! I recommend serving this with a ton of grilled sourdough bread. Your guests will want to sop up every drop of that broth!

Chef Amanda's Seafood Prep Tips

Keep all of your proteins separate, and when you've finished prepping them, store them in the fridge.

- **To clean clams and mussels:** Rinse the clams and mussels separately under cold running water for approximately 10 minutes.
- **To clean shrimp:** Remove the shells from the shrimp and reserve them for the stock. (You can buy cleaned shrimp, which is a little less work, but your soup stock will really benefit from having the shells.) Once you've removed the shells from your shrimp, take a small knife and run it along the backside of the shrimp, from top to tail, and remove the black vein.
- **To break down a lobster:** There are several ways to go about this. I recommend using your hands wrapped in a towel to remove the claws and tail from the body. You can break open the tail with your hands and use a meat pounder to gently tap the claws to remove the meat from them. Save all of your shells and the head!! To clean the head, lift the top part off of the body and rinse out all of the green gooey stuff. You'll notice that there are gills attached to the body. These are easy to pull off with your hands.
- **To break down a crab:** Lift off the head, cut the body in half lengthwise and then cut it in between each leg so that you have a leg attached to a chunk of the body for each of your guests.

desse

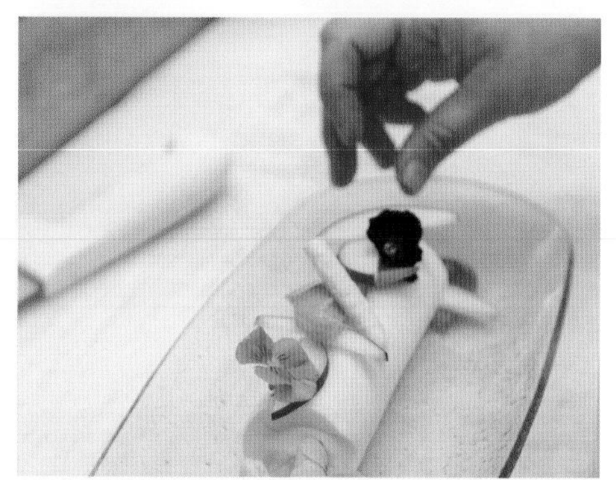

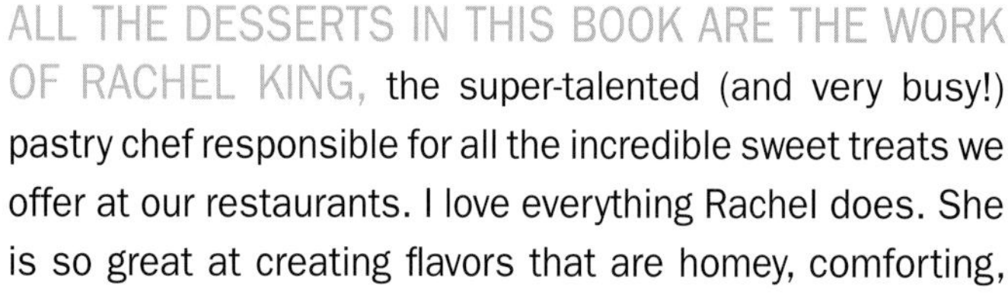

ALL THE DESSERTS IN THIS BOOK ARE THE WORK OF RACHEL KING, the super-talented (and very busy!) pastry chef responsible for all the incredible sweet treats we offer at our restaurants. I love everything Rachel does. She is so great at creating flavors that are homey, comforting, delicious, and interesting — all at the same time! She can also do sophisticated and elegant. Her desserts are world class and she covers such a broad range of styles! Her take on sweets is the same as my take on everything else. Go with the classic things that people love to eat, put your special spin on them, make them extraordinary, and make them your own! (But whatever you do, don't ask her about the Caddy Shack "Pool Bar" or doing a strawberry fan. She may be cute, but this *chica* will cut you!)

Chef Rachel King

When the whole adventure started, I put some ads out for a pastry chef. There were a few people in town that I had my eye on, and one of them was this darling young girl named Rachel King. She had been working for Jack Fisher at NINE-TEN (Jack being arguably one of the best pastry chefs in San Diego) and she had been there for a long time. Rachel was exactly the kind of person I was looking for: young, motivated, coming up in the industry. So, she came in, looked at my menu at Searsucker, and that night wrote me a dessert menu. I read it the next day, and it was absolutely perfect. It was exactly what I wanted — taking the classics and having some fun with them, twisting them up and going for it (she put bacon in a caramel sauce for dessert! Forget it! Right there, she had me!). The fact is that she's so organized, so professional, so disciplined that she can read one of my menus and the next day I'll have a collection of desserts that are spot on. Boom. Done. It's amazing, but somehow she manages to keep up with us. I don't know how she does it, I'm just glad she does.

olive brittle

serves 8 friends

I'm a total sucker for really sweet desserts, but Chef Rachel has gotten me to appreciate the greatness of desserts that mix sweet and salty. That's why this concoction is one of Rachel's most addicting. If you're more of a traditionalist, you can always use nuts instead of the olives, but c'mon, you got to try the olives at least once! And try breaking some of this up and mixing it into your favorite ice cream! It's a toe curler!

½ cup olives, pitted and chopped (I like Kalamata or black Italian)
½ cup water
1 cup granulated sugar
½ cup light corn syrup
1 tablespoon butter
1 teaspoon baking soda (this is the secret ingredient — it aerates!)

[how to do it]

1. Preheat oven to 300°F.
2. Put the olives on a small sheet tray or pan and bake them until they are dry, about 1 hour.
3. In a medium saucepan on high heat, combine the water, sugar, and corn syrup. Cook the mixture until it turns a golden brown, about 8 to 10 minutes.
4. Stir in the butter. Continue cooking until the butter is melted and thoroughly incorporated. Take off heat and stir in the baking soda.
5. Stir in the olives and immediately pour the mixture out onto a Silpat (silicon baking sheet) or a greased sheet pan and flatten with another Silpat or a layer of wax paper and a rolling pin.
6. Once the brittle has cooled completely, break it into bite-sized pieces. You can store this in an airtight container for up to 1 week.

searsucker's apple + ale muffins

makes 12 muffins

Who doesn't want more ways to get beer into breakfast? This is one of Chef Rachel's newest creations, and they're everything you want in a muffin: The beer adds a really nice, delicate and airy texture to these, with a tender crumb and chunks of apple in every bite.

1 stick (4 ounces) + 3 tablespoons butter
3 apples (I like Granny Smith, but Galas or Empires would work — you want firm apples with good acidity), peeled, cored, and diced into medium chunks
1 cup light brown sugar
1 egg
1½ cups all-purpose flour
1 teaspoon baking powder
½ teaspoon baking soda
½ teaspoon ground cinnamon
Pinch kosher salt
1 cup malty beer (my favorite is AleSmith's Nautical Nut Brown)

[how to do it]

1. Preheat oven to 325°F. Line muffin pans with paper cups or just grease them.
2. In a large sauté pan, melt 3 tablespoons of the butter and sauté the apples until soft (about 10 to 15 minutes). Set aside.
3. In a mixing bowl, cream together the remaining butter and brown sugar until fluffy. Add the egg and beat until combined.
4. In a medium bowl, whisk the dry ingredients together. Mix the dry mixture into the butter mixture until there are no lumps and everything is incorporated. Stir in the beer and fold in the apples. Fill muffin tins about ¾ of the way up and bake for about 15 minutes. Test for doneness by poking a toothpick in the center of the cakes — it should come out with just a few crumbs attached. Cool completely before serving.

cashew + coconut caramel corn

serves 6 friends

I can't get enough of caramel corn! Salty, sweet, buttery — it has it all! And it's one of those desserts that reminds you of the simple pleasures of the past somehow. Chef Rachel has used this as a garnish on many of her desserts. If you want to make it even more decadent (of course you do!), you can drizzle the caramel corn with some melted chocolate when it has cooled. You can also sub out any kind of nut you like, and you can add other flavors and textures to it — this recipe is made with coconut and it's AWESOME!

½ cup corn kernels (use packaged popping corn)
2 tablespoons canola oil
½ cup cashews, peanuts, or your favorite nut, chopped into large pieces
½ cup shredded coconut
1 cup granulated sugar
¼ cup corn syrup
½ cup water
1 tablespoon butter
1 tablespoon sea salt
2 teaspoons baking soda

[how to do it]

1. Put the corn in a medium pot with 2 tablespoons oil and cover. (Or, if you are lucky enough to have a popcorn popper, use according to directions.) Make sure to shake the pot frequently and to keep the heat high, but not too high. Remove the pot from the heat when the popping stops. (Be careful: Don't take the lid off before the popping stops or you will have popcorn flying everywhere!)
2. Pour the popcorn into a heat-safe bowl that has been coated with nonstick spray or rubbed with butter. Mix in cashews and coconut.
3. In a medium saucepot on high heat, combine the sugar, corn syrup, and water and cook until it turns a deep golden brown, about 8 minutes. Watch it carefully: sugar goes from light tan to burned very quickly! Mix in the butter and salt until completely combined. Take off the heat and stir in the baking soda until completely combined.
4. Immediately pour the caramel over the popcorn and stir well, to evenly coat the popcorn. Pour the mix out onto a sheet tray (buttered or lined with a Silpat) and, once it is slightly cooled, put on gloves and break it apart into pieces (and try not to eat it all before you're done!). Once it has cooled completely, store in an airtight container for up to 1 week.

"I think people love caramel corn because it reminds them of great memories, like your first box of Cracker Jack or the freshly made kettle corn you used to get at the country fair. I love making desserts that bring back happy memories like that."
— Chef Rachel

doughnuts + espresso chocolate sauce

makes 30 doughnut holes

Once you have a freshly fried homemade doughnut, you'll never go back to buying them in a store! These are so rich and delicious, and so easy — especially when you have some warm chocolate sauce to dip them in! Fresh out of the fryer! Don't accept anything less! You can keep this dough in the freezer for up to 1 month and thaw it out when you want to fry up some sweet, hot balls of goodness!

[for the dough]
1 teaspoon instant dry yeast
1 cup milk
⅓ cup granulated sugar
2½ cups all-purpose flour
1 egg
Pinch kosher salt
¼ stick (1 ounce) butter
½ stick (2 ounces) shortening
(I prefer Crisco baking sticks)

[for the chocolate sauce]
½ cup heavy cream
½ cup espresso or strong coffee
½ cup granulated sugar
8 ounces dark chocolate, chopped

[for cooking the doughnuts]
2 to 3 cups canola oil, for pan or deep frying
Cinnamon and sugar, for coating

[how to do it]

1. Make the dough: Put the yeast in the bowl of a stand mixer. In a small saucepan, warm the milk to just above room temperature. Be careful not to get it too hot or it will kill the yeast and your doughnuts will not rise. Pour the milk over the yeast and let it sit for 3 to 5 minutes.
2. Add the remaining ingredients to the mixing bowl and mix with a dough hook until the mixture is silky and smooth, with no lumps, about 10 minutes. Cover the dough and let it rest (proof) for 1 hour.
3. On a clean, floured work surface, use a rolling pin to roll the dough out to a 1-inch thickness (the dough should be quite springy, wet, and sticky — you can roll it in a little flour to make it easier to work with, if necessary). Use a 1-inch diameter cookie cutter to cut doughnut holes. If you don't have cookie cutters, you can simply cut the doughnuts into squares.
4. Make the sauce: In a medium saucepan, combine the cream, espresso, and sugar and bring to a boil, stirring constantly to dissolve the sugar. Place the chocolate pieces in a medium bowl. Pour the hot liquid over the dark chocolate and whisk until smooth and shiny. Serve warm or reheat before serving.
5. Fry the dough: In a skillet or deep fryer, heat the oil to 375°F. Fry until the doughnuts are a dark golden brown (don't take them out too early!). Toss them in cinnamon and sugar and let cool for a minute before serving with warm chocolate sauce.

red velvet sandwich cookies

makes 16 sandwich cookies

Who doesn't love a great cookie? These cookies are soft and chewy. They're great on their own, if you don't want to take the extra step to sandwich them with the frosting (but you'd be crazy not to). Chef Rachel makes the world's best mini ice cream sandwiches with these! Whoopie! I love 'em! She serves them with her ever-so-popular red velvet cake and our customers can't get enough of them! The people have spoken!

[for the dough]

3 sticks (12 ounces) butter
2 cups granulated sugar
2 eggs
1 tablespoon pure vanilla extract
2 tablespoons red food coloring (beet juice works, too)
2½ cups all-purpose flour
½ cup cocoa powder
½ teaspoon baking soda
1 teaspoon kosher salt

[for the frosting]

2 cups white chocolate, chopped
2 sticks (8 ounces) butter, at room temperature
8 ounces cream cheese, at room temperature

[how to do it]

1. Preheat oven to 325°F.
2. **Make the dough:** In a stand mixer with the paddle attachment, cream together the butter and sugar until light and fluffy. Add the eggs one by one and beat until combined. Add the vanilla and the food coloring.
3. In a bowl, whisk together the dry ingredients and add to the butter mixture. Beat until combined.
4. Use an ice cream scoop to shape the cookies. (If you don't have any scoops, just use a spoon and shape the cookies by hand about the size of ping pong balls.) Bake on a greased sheet tray for about 10 minutes, until the edges are firm, but the centers are still soft (be careful not to overbake these). The cookies will continue cooking after they come out of the oven. Cool completely before sandwiching.
5. **Make the frosting:** Melt the chocolate over a double boiler or in a microwave (on low). Make sure not to burn it! Set aside. In a stand mixer with the paddle attachment, beat the butter and cream cheese together until smooth and fluffy. Beat in the melted chocolate until combined.
6. Assemble sandwiches by placing a spoonful of frosting on one cookie and topping with another cookie.

carrot cake + ginger cream cheese frosting

serves 8 to 12 friends

In the restaurant biz, you learn a lot about people's tastes and eating habits. One thing I've learned is that people either LOVE or HATE carrot cake. I obviously fall into the former category! I could eat this cake for breakfast, lunch, and dinner. But even if you are unsure of your feelings for carrot cake, try this out. People who "don't like carrot cake" still seem to love this recipe. It's a little lighter than a traditional carrot cake and it has a slight spicy tropical flavor from the ginger cream cheese frosting.

[for the batter]
1 cup canola oil
2 cups granulated sugar
½ cup buttermilk
4 eggs
Pinch kosher salt
2 cups all-purpose flour
1 tablespoon baking soda
1 tablespoon ground cinnamon
Pinch nutmeg
Pinch ground ginger
2 cups grated carrot

[for the frosting]
2 sticks (8 ounces) butter
1 pound (16 ounces) cream cheese
1 cup powdered sugar
1 tablespoon grated fresh ginger

[finishing touches]
Whipped cream
Fresh fruit pieces
Edible flowers

[how to do it]

1. Preheat oven to 325°F. Butter and flour an 8-by-12-inch baking pan.
2. Make the batter: In a medium bowl, whisk together the oil, sugar, buttermilk, and eggs.
3. In another medium bowl, whisk together the remaining dry ingredients. Mix the dry mixture into the wet mixture until it is well incorporated (there are no lumps).
4. Fold in the carrots. Pour the batter into the prepared baking pan and bake for about 25 minutes. Test for doneness by inserting a toothpick into the center of the cake — it should come out clean. Allow cake to cool completely.
5. Make the frosting: Bring the butter to room temperature. Using a stand mixer, beat all the ingredients together until the frosting is smooth and fluffy. Spread onto the cake. You can leave the frosting as is, or top it with any variety of your favorite toppings (I love coconut, walnuts, cashews, mango, or edible flowers like violets).

lemon poppyseed cake

serves 12 friends

This cake is so popular at Gingham! We fill it with jam and lemon mousse at the restaurant, but I also think it's great with just a simple glaze over the top. It has a light lemon flavor and an airy texture. It's so light, I'm always surprised that night after night it's one of our most popular desserts — a crowd pleaser for sure!

[for the batter]
3 cups all-purpose flour
1 tablespoon baking soda
Pinch kosher salt
½ cup poppy seeds
1½ cups canola oil
2½ cups granulated sugar
2 cups buttermilk
3 eggs
2 tablespoons lemon zest
½ cup freshly squeezed lemon juice

[for the glaze]
1 cup powdered sugar
1 tablespoon freshly squeezed lemon juice
2 tablespoons milk

[how to do it]

1. Preheat oven to 325°F. Grease an 8-by-14-inch baking pan.
2. **Prepare the batter:** In a medium bowl, sift the flour together with the baking soda and salt and mix in the poppy seeds.
3. In a medium bowl, whisk together the oil, sugar, buttermilk, eggs, and zest. Stir in the dry ingredients and mix until all of the lumps are gone. Whisk in the lemon juice and pour in the pan immediately.
4. Bake for 20 minutes, or until a tester or skewer comes out clean. Allow the cake to cool.
5. **Make the glaze:** In a small bowl, whisk the ingredients together and pour it evenly over the cake. Let the glaze set for 1 hour before slicing and serving.

key lime pie

makes 1 (8-inch) pie

Here's a super fast and easy recipe you can do without spending a lot of time in the kitchen. This key lime pie is creamy and smooth with just the right touch of citrus tang. It's light, refreshing, not too sweet, and perfect for a hot summer evening.

[for the custard]
2 cups + 1 tablespoon condensed milk
1 cup heavy cream
1 cup (about 12) egg yolks
1½ cups freshly squeezed key lime juice

[for the crust]
1 store-bought, prebaked graham cracker crust

[finishing touches]
Whipped cream
Edible flowers

[how to do it]

Chef's note: Either buy a graham cracker crust and bake it according to package directions or make it even easier on yourself: purchase a prebaked one from the supermarket. Work on the filling once the crust is prepared.

1. Preheat oven to 300°F.
2. **Make the custard:** In a large bowl, whisk together the milk, cream, and yolks. Whisk in the juice and combine well. Pour the custard into premade crust.
3. **Bake the pie:** Bake for about 45 minutes, until the custard stops jiggling. Chill for 4 hours before serving.
4. Serve slices with whipped cream and edible flowers.

lemon mousse

serves 6 friends

People LOVE lemon desserts! This mousse is incredibly light and airy. Chef Rachel uses it at a few of the restaurants, and in a bunch of different ways. It can stand on its own, but it also makes a great cake filling, cookie accompaniment, or tart filling. It's that perfect amount of citrus sweetness for when you're not in the mood for anything heavy — and it pairs beautifully with just about any kind of berry or fresh fruit.

[for the mousse]
½ cup water
2 tablespoons gelatin
1½ sticks (6 ounces) butter
1 cup freshly squeezed lemon juice
4 eggs
1 cup granulated sugar
1 cup heavy whipping cream

[finishing touches]
Edible flowers
Fresh mixed berries

[how to do it]

1. Start the mousse: In a small bowl, mix the water and gelatin and set aside.
2. In a saucepan, melt the butter over medium-high heat and then add the lemon juice. Add the eggs and the sugar, whisking vigorously until the mixture starts to thicken.
3. Stir in the gelatin mixture and whisk until it is well incorporated. Strain the mixture through a fine mesh sieve and chill in an ice bath until cool to the touch, stirring frequently, about 10 minutes. Chill in the fridge, about 30 minutes.
4. Whip the cream to soft peaks by hand or with whisk attachment on a stand mixer (so that when you put your whisk in it and take it out, the cream barely holds its shape). Fold the whipped cream into the cold lemon mixture. Spoon the mousse into glasses or pour into ring molds and chill for at least 1 hour before serving.
5. To serve: Unmold the mousse from the rings or serve in the glasses. Garnish with edible flowers and berries.

lemon bars

makes 8 bars

We call these "Pucker Bars" at Searsucker because of their tart punch! What a great blast of big ol' lemon flavor sitting on top of that buttery crust! You sink your teeth into this and get all the crumble and smooth happening in your mouth in one big citrus explosion! Plenty of tart, sour, lemony goodness makes these sing! Customers love these because they're a great interpretation of the classic bake sale standard we all remember and loved.

[for the crust]
1½ cups all-purpose flour
½ cup powdered sugar
2 sticks (8 ounces) butter, cold, and cut into ½-inch pieces

[for the filling]
7 eggs
2½ cups granulated sugar
½ cup all-purpose flour
1½ cups freshly squeezed lemon juice

[finishing touches]
Powdered sugar
Fresh mixed berries

[how to do it]

1. Preheat oven to 325°F.
2. **Make the crust:** In a bowl, mix all the ingredients together until the mixture becomes crumbly. Press the dough into a square 8-by-8-inch baking pan (greased or lined with parchment) and bake until golden brown, about 15 to 20 minutes.
3. Lower oven temperature to 300°F.
4. **Make the filling:** In a stand mixer, beat the eggs and sugar until the mixture becomes a little fluffy. Add the flour and mix until well combined. Add the lemon juice and mix until the mixture is smooth.
5. Pour the filling mix over the cooled crust and bake for 30 minutes, or until the center is set.
6. Refrigerate for 2 to 3 hours, until the filling is set.
7. **To serve:** Cut into squares, top with powdered sugar, and pucker up!

"Personally, I think these are the best lemon bars ever. A lot of bars don't have enough filling, so they're kind of dry. These have what I think is the perfect filling-to-crust ratio. And they're also not super, over-the-top sweet, which, in my opinion, is very important."
— Chef Rachel

coconut-filled brownies

makes 16 sandwich cookies

We serve this as our birthday dessert at Burlap (it's actually not on the menu — you have to ask for it and give us the secret handshake). People go crazy for these! It's like having a giant turbo-charged Mounds bar in your mouth — a chocolate bomb with a coconut blast! We often have customers asking for more and asking to purchase them to go. And you wouldn't believe how many birthdays some people can have in one year!

[for the filling]
4 cups coconut, shredded
1 can (14 ounces) condensed milk
1 cup milk

[for the batter]
2 sticks (8 ounces) butter
2 cups granulated sugar
4 eggs
1 tablespoon pure vanilla extract
2 cups all-purpose flour
½ cup cocoa powder
1 teaspoon baking powder
Pinch kosher salt

[how to do it]

1. Preheat oven to 325°F. Grease an 8-by-14-inch baking pan.
2. **Make the filling:** In a medium bowl, stir together the ingredients and set aside.
3. **Make the batter:** In a stand mixer with the paddle attachment, cream together the butter and sugar until light and fluffy. Add the eggs one by one and beat until combined. Add the vanilla.
4. In a medium bowl, whisk together the dry ingredients to combine well and add them to the butter mixture. Beat on slow speed until well combined.
5. Spread two-thirds of the batter evenly onto the bottom of the pan. Spread the coconut filling evenly over the batter. Top with the remaining brownie batter — it will be thin, but you just want to cover all the coconut so it does not burn. Bake for about 20 minutes, until the edges are firm but the center is still soft. Let cool completely before serving — unless you want to serve it warm with ice cream. It's way messier that way, but it's sooooo good!

strawberry-rhubarb crumble

serves 4 to 6 friends

Very few things can beat a fresh-out-of-the-oven fruit crumble. I love making crumbles at home because they are so easy and fill my house with the most amazing smell! Strawberry-rhubarb has been the most popular fruit combination we have had at Searsucker (sweet and sour deliciousness!), but switch it up, get creative, stretch yourself — and use what's in season. Some of my favorite combinations are apple-cranberry, pear-huckleberry, pear-blackberry, and cherry-nectarine. The list goes on and on! Just make sure to adjust the sugar to how sweet the different types of fruit are and reduce the cornstarch if the fruit is not as juicy.

[for the topping]
1 cup all-purpose flour
1 cup rolled oats
¾ cup light brown sugar
¾ cup granulated sugar
2 sticks (8 ounces) butter, cut into small pea-sized cubes, chilled

[for the filling]
2 cups granulated sugar
2½ pounds fresh strawberries, stems cut off and quartered
2 pounds rhubarb, ends cut off, unripe sections trimmed, cut into ⅓-inch pieces
3 tablespoons cornstarch

[finishing touches]
Ice cream
Whipped cream
Whipped mascarpone, crème fraîche, or sour cream

[how to do it]

1. Preheat oven to 350°F.
2. Make the topping: In a large bowl, mix all of the ingredients together with your hands. Use your fingertips to work the butter into the flour until it is the size of tiny pebbles. Set aside.
3. Make the filling: In a medium bowl, toss all the ingredients together to combine and coat well. Pour into a shallow baking dish. Completely cover the fruit with the crumble topping and bake for 40 minutes, or until the top of the crumble is golden brown and the bubbles in the liquid are a thick syrup consistency.
4. Cool for 10 minutes before serving warm. Serve with the ice cream of your choice or just by itself.

sea salt blondies

makes 16 pieces

This is our non-chocolate version of our fudge brownies. They're dense, rich, chewy, and so satisfying (I'm satisfied after about three!). The extra sprinkling of sea salt is important to balance out the sweetness of the brown sugar. If you need a little pick-me-up, these make great afternoon treats. Of course, there are oh so many uses for these — like folding them into ice cream. At Herringbone we put chunks of blondies in our ice cream sundae and it's crazy good!

3¾ sticks (15 ounces) butter, melted
4 cups brown sugar, firmly packed
5 eggs
2 tablespoons pure vanilla extract
½ teaspoon kosher salt
3 cups all-purpose flour
1 teaspoon baking powder
1 tablespoon sea salt

[how to do it]

1. Preheat oven to 325°F. Grease an 8-by-12-inch baking dish.
2. In a medium bowl, whisk together the butter and brown sugar until the mixture is smooth. Add the eggs one by one and beat until well combined. Add the vanilla and the salt.
3. In a medium bowl, whisk together the flour and baking powder and add to the butter mixture. Stir until combined. Pour into the pan and sprinkle with sea salt.
4. Bake for about 15 minutes, until the edges are set but the center is just a little wet looking. Do not overbake or they will not reach their maximum delicious potential! Let cool.
5. Eat them plain, frost them, or break them up and stir them into your favorite ice cream.

"I'm a big fan of desserts like brownies and bars — the berry bars, in particular, are so easy to pick up and eat and they're very satisfying. They have a great, homey, berry flavor that really shines through!"
— Chef Rachel

berry pie bars

makes 12 bars

This is a dessert I love to whip up at home — I love to keep it around for lunch and snacks, and you can cut them up and bring them anywhere (bars at the beach, anyone?). This is another recipe for you to run with on your own. Go to the farmers market and find a bunch of great, local fruit in season and go insane! Mix it up, throw it together with the pie bar crust, and you've got it goin' on!

[for the crust]
1½ sticks (6 ounces) butter
¾ cup + 1 tablespoon (6 ounces) shortening (I prefer Crisco)
2 tablespoons granulated sugar
1 tablespoon kosher salt
3 cups all-purpose flour
½ cup rolled oats
3 tablespoons water

[for the filling]
4 eggs
2 cups granulated sugar
1 cup sour cream
¾ cup all-purpose flour
Pinch kosher salt
1 cup blackberries
1 cup raspberries
1 cup blueberries

[how to do it]

1. Preheat oven to 325°F.
2. Make the crust: In a large bowl, mix all the ingredients together by hand, except for the water. Break up the fats with your fingers until the mixture has a pebbly texture. Mix in the water and work until the dough comes together slightly.
3. Press three-quarters of the dough into a greased 9-by-13-inch baking dish. Reserve the unused dough. Bake for about 12 minutes, until the crust is a light golden brown. Remove from oven (leave the temperature set).
4. Make the filling: In a large bowl, whisk together the eggs, sugar, and sour cream. Whisk in flour and salt.
5. Gently fold the berries into the mixture and pour over the crust. Crumble the remaining dough over the filling and bake for about 40 minutes, until the center jiggles only slightly when moved. Chill until cold and firm. Cut when cold.

condensed milk cake

serves 12 friends

This is Burlap's version of the classic* tres leches*, with a little of its own Latino swagger. The density and chewiness of this cake is what I love the most. It's got such delicate flavors, but the texture and heft give it real personality. This is the "most interesting cake in the world," my friends!

[for the batter]
2 sticks (8 ounces) butter
1 cup granulated sugar
4 eggs
1 teaspoon pure vanilla extract
1 cup condensed milk
½ cup buttermilk
2 cups all-purpose flour
Pinch kosher salt
1 teaspoon baking powder
½ teaspoon baking soda

[for the soak]
½ cup milk
1 cup condensed milk
½ cup heavy cream

[finishing touches]
Caramel
Kumquats and/or other tart citrus

[how to do it]

1. Preheat oven to 325°F. Grease an 8-by-14-inch pan.
2. **Make the batter:** In a stand mixer, cream the butter and sugar until light and fluffy. Add the eggs one by one and then add the vanilla. Add the condensed milk and buttermilk and beat for 1 minute.
3. In a mixing bowl, combine the remaining dry ingredients. Fold the dry ingredients into the wet and pour the batter into the baking pan. Bake for about 25 minutes, turning half way through. Test for doneness by inserting a tester or skewer. Cake is done if it comes out clean.
4. Remove the cake from the oven and poke holes in the top of the cake with a wooden skewer or similar.
5. **Make the soak:** In a small bowl, whisk together the soak ingredients. Slowly pour the soak over the top of the cake and let it cool completely before slicing and serving with your favorite ice cream and toppings.

vietnamese coffee ice cream

makes 6 cups

Homemade ice cream is such a great treat. This flavor is a huge seller at Burlap and it's awesome as a topping on just about anything — even waffles for breakfast!

2 cups milk
1 cup heavy cream
3 tablespoons coffee powder
Pinch kosher salt
9 egg yolks
2 cups condensed milk

[how to do it]

Chef's note: You'll need an ice cream maker to make your own ice cream. And if you want to make frozen scoops of ice cream, you'll need to start this several hours before serving. Otherwise, you can make a soft-serve treat within an hour or two.

1. In a medium saucepot on medium heat, scald the milk (heat to just below boiling) and add the cream, coffee powder, and salt, stirring constantly.
2. Put the yolks in a bowl and whisk in a bit of the hot milk to temper (heat the yolks gently).
3. Whisk the tempered yolks into the hot milk and keep whisking until it thickens slightly (be careful not to scramble!). Strain through a fine mesh sieve. Whisk in the condensed milk and refrigerate until completely chilled (about an hour).
4. Churn in an ice cream maker according to the manufacturer's instructions.
5. Serve with your favorite nuts, sauces, or toppings (the possibilities are endless!).

chocolate puddin'

serves 6 friends

Every person has a few desserts that bring them back to happy memories from childhood — and Chef Rachel loves doing desserts that have that nostalgic effect. She used to always look forward to the pudding cups she would get in her lunch box, so she developed a richer, more adult version that creates happy memories every time you eat it! It also makes a dynamite pie or cake filling. Whipped cream? Sh*t yeah! Choco-junkies unite!

[for the candied nuts]
2 egg whites
2 cups nuts, use your favorite kind
1 cup granulated sugar

[for the pudding]
2 cups milk
½ cup granulated sugar
4 egg yolks (reserve the whites for the candied nuts)

⅓ cup (1½ ounces) cornstarch
7 ounces dark (bittersweet) good-quality chocolate (I like Scharffen Berger, Lindt, or Ghirardelli)
½ stick (2 ounces) butter, cut into small pea-sized cubes

[finishing touches]
Whipped cream
Chocolate shavings (optional)

[how to do it]

1. Preheat oven to 350°F.
2. **Make the candied nuts:** In a medium bowl, whisk the whites until frothy and add the nuts. Stir to mix well. With a slotted spoon, transfer the nuts to a bowl with the sugar and toss well to coat. Spread the nuts out on a greased sheet tray and bake until golden brown, about 12 to 15 minutes. Allow to cool.
3. **Make the pudding:** In a medium saucepot on medium heat, scald the milk.
4. In a medium mixing bowl, whisk together the sugar, yolks, and cornstarch. Add a little of the hot milk to the mixing bowl, whisking quickly to temper the eggs and warm them (without cooking them).
5. Add the egg mixture to the milk and bring to a boil, whisking constantly.
6. Remove from the heat and whisk in the chocolate and the butter, combining well. Pour into a stand mixer and beat until the mixture has nearly cooled to room temperature. Spoon into serving dishes and chill to set.
7. Serve with the candied nuts, whipped cream, or chocolate shavings on top.

vanilla bean ice cream

makes 1 quart

Here's our basic vanilla ice cream recipe (the secret with vanilla is to use a real vanilla bean). It's a blank canvas to use to create your masterpiece. Don't limit yourself to vanilla, though, because this recipe is really versatile. You can change up the flavors by simply infusing the milk with other ingredients. Some ideas? How about earl grey, jasmine, Grand Marnier, hazelnut, or cinnamon?

2 cups milk
2 cups heavy cream
1 vanilla bean, split in half lengthwise
6 egg yolks
1¼ cups granualted sugar
Pinch kosher salt

[how to do it]

Chef's note: You'll need an ice cream maker to make your own ice cream. And if you want to make frozen scoops of ice cream, you'll need to start this several hours before serving. Otherwise, you can make a soft-serve treat within an hour or two.

1. In a medium pot, scald the milk and cream with the vanilla bean (scrape out the seeds from inside the bean before dropping the two halves into the milk).
2. In a medium bowl, whisk together the yolks, sugar, and salt.
3. Temper the yolks by pouring about ½ cup of the milk mixture into the yolk mixture, while whisking constantly. Add the yolk mixture to the hot milk/cream and put it all back on medium heat. Cook until thickened slightly (this is your basic crème anglaise). Press the yolk mixture through a chinois, or fine strainer into a bowl on top of an ice bath. Allow to cool.
4. Churn in an ice cream maker, according to manufacturer's directions.
5. Serve with your favorite toppings.

drinks

Lucien (left) and Ian

ALL THE COCKTAILS FOR OUR RESTAURANTS ARE THE ORIGINAL CREATIONS OF LUCIEN CONNER AND IAN WARD. They've recently added Jen Queen to the their team, and together they provide us with the really fun, interesting, and totally unique drinks that people love at our restaurants. They're really into the idea of "progressive cocktails" that are not just big, syrupy sweet bombs. They make all their own simple syrups and they do all their own infusions. We have popcorn margaritas now, we've got cucumber vodkas, you name it. They're just constantly pushing the envelope with our drink menu and they've gained a real cult following here. It's just one of those magic things. When you've got a great restaurant, great cooks, great chefs, great GMs, great wait staff, great ambiance, and you have those perfect cocktails, it just ties the whole thing together so perfectly.

burlap julep

makes 1 cocktail

[for the lychee-demerara syrup]
1 cup water
1 cup demerara sugar
1 cup fresh mint leaves
1 cup lychee syrup (strain the canned fruit and reserve for garnish)
½ cup freshly squeezed lemon juice
½ cup St. Germain elderflower liquor

[finishing touches]
2 ounces bourbon
4 leaves fresh mint

[how to do it]

1. Make the lychee syrup: In a medium pot on medium heat, combine the water, sugar, and mint and whisk until all the sugar is dissolved. Remove from the heat and strain out the mint leaves. Allow the mixture to cool. Add the lychee syrup, lemon juice, and the elderflower liquor.
2. In a cocktail shaker full of cubed ice combine the bourbon and ¼ ounce of Lychee-Demerera syrup.
3. Shake thoroughly and strain into a rocks glass overflowing with crushed ice.
4. Garnish with a reserved peeled lychee and fresh mint that has been lightly whipped back and forth across your palm a few times.

the dragon

makes 1 cocktail

[for the dragon mix]
2 cups distilled white vinegar
2 ounces dried Japanese chiles
6 cans Foco Mangosteen Juice
1 cup granulated sugar
½ cup freshly squeezed lemon juice
Pinch celery salt

[finishing touches]
¾ ounce tequila
2½ ounces prosecco
Red chiles

[how to do it]

1. Make the dragon mix: In a medium pot combine the vinegar, chiles, Mangosteen Juice, sugar, lemon juice, and celery salt. Put the stockpot on the stove, bring to a boil, then reduce heat to medium and let cook for 10 minutes. Remove from heat and allow to cool. Once cooled, strain the liquid through a fine mesh sieve, making sure no peppers or pepper seeds are left in the liquid. Keep refrigerated in an airtight container.

2. Pour 1½ ounces of dragon mix into a champagne flute, then fill with tequila and Prosecco. Garnish with red chiles.

coyote

makes 1 cocktail

[for the cinnamon bourbon]

1 cinnamon stick
1 (1-liter) bottle bourbon

[finishing touches]

1 ounce freshly squeezed lime juice
3 ounces ginger beer
2 dashes bitters
Cinnamon sticks
Fresh lime wheel

[how to do it]

1. Make the cinnamon bourbon: Add the cinnamon stick to the bottle of bourbon. Allow the cinnamon and bourbon to infuse at room temperature for 24 hours, then refrigerate.

2. In a Collins glass, first add 2 ounces of the cinnamon bourbon, then the lime juice, ginger beer, and top off with the bitters. Stir. Garnish with cinnamon sticks and, if desired, a lime wheel.

peter rabbit

makes 1 cocktail

[for the simple syrup]
3 cups sugar
3 cups water
Pinch salt

[for the basil-lemon]
1 tablespoon fresh basil leaves
1 cup freshly squeezed lemon juice

[finishing touches]
2 ounces Pimm's
Pickled carrot
Fresh basil leaf

[how to do it]

1. **Make the simple syrup:** In a pot on medium heat, whisk the ingredients until all the sugar is dissolved. Let cool.
2. **Make the basil-lemon:** Combine the ingredients in a blender and blend on high for 1 minute. Strain to remove any solids.
3. In a shaker, combine the Pimm's with 1 ounce of basil-lemon, and 1 ounce of simple syrup over ice. Shake, and strain into a rocks glass with ice. Garnish with a pickled carrot and basil leaf.

the cock

makes 1 cocktail

[for the simple syrup]
3 cups sugar
3 cups water
Pinch salt

[for the cucumber water]
3 cucumbers, peeled, halved, sliced into 2-inch segments
Water, as needed
2 teaspoons wasabi paste

[finishing touches]
1½ ounces vodka
¼ ounce freshly squeezed lemon juice
1 cucumber slice

[how to do it]

1. Make the simple syrup: In a pot on medium heat, whisk the ingredients until all the sugar is dissolved. Let cool.
2. Make the cucumber water: Place cucumber slices in a blender and fill remainder with water. Process until completely liquified. Strain, and whisk in the wasabi. Keep refrigerated in an airtight container.
3. In a cocktail shaker, combine the vodka, 1 ounce of cucumber water, lemon juice, and ¼ ounce of simple syrup.
4. Add ice to the shaker, shake, and strain into a martini glass. Garnish with cucumber.

the rat aka the 'popcorn margarita'

makes 1 cocktail

[for the popcorn tequila]
1 cup buttered popcorn
1 (1-liter) bottle tequila

[finishing touches]
1 ounce freshly squeezed lime juice
1 ounce agave nectar
Lime wedge

[how to do it]

1. Make the popcorn tequila: In a glass container, combine the popcorn and tequila. Allow the popcorn and tequila to infuse refrigerated, for a minimum of 4 hours.
2. Combine 2 ounces of popcorn tequila with the lime juice and agave in a mixing glass with ice. Shake and strain into a salt- rimmed rocks glass with ice.
3. Garnish with lime wedge and a dried corn husk tied in a knot.

gabby bloody mary

makes 1 cocktail

[for the gabby mudd]
4 ounces extra-hot horseradish
4 ounces Frank's Red Hot sauce
5 ounces Worcestershire sauce
2 cloves fresh garlic, crushed
2 stalks celery, diced
2 tablespoons kosher salt
2 tablespoons freshly ground black pepper
2 tablespoons celery salt
½ red onion, diced

[for the house stock]
12 corncobs (kernels removed)
4 peppercorns
2 stems fresh parsley
2 stems fresh thyme
1 bay leaf

[for the gabby mix]
2 cups beer (preferably an IPA)
½ cup freshly squeezed lime juice
1 (28-ounce) can whole peeled tomatoes with juice

[finishing touches]
1½ ounces vodka
Celery stalk, olive, lime wedge, hot pepper, carrot

[how to do it]

1. Make the gabby mudd: Combine all the ingredients in small batches in a blender. In a large container, whisk the small batches together. Keep refrigerated in an airtight container.
2. Make the house stock: In a large pot, combine all the ingredients in 14 cups of cold water and bring to a boil over high heat. Reduce heat to medium and simmer for 1½ hours. Strain, discard solids, and refrigerate or freeze until ready to use.
3. Make the gabby mix: In a container, combine 2 cups house stock, ½ cup gabby mudd and remaining gabby mix ingredients. Mix well and refrigerate until needed.
4. Make the bloody: In a salt- and pepper-rimmed tall glass, combine vodka with gabby mix. Garnish with celery stalk, olive, hot pepper, carrot, and lime wedge.

contact us

[**BRIAN MALARKEY**] www.brianmalarkey.com

[**BURLAP**] 12995 El Camino Real, Suite 21, Del Mar, CA 92130, (858) 369-5700, www.burlapeats.com

[**GABARDINE**] 1005 Rosecrans Street, San Diego, CA 92106, (619) 398-9810, www.gabardineeats.com

[**GINGHAM**] 8384 La Mesa Boulevard, La Mesa, CA 91942, (619) 797-1922, www.ginghameats.com

[**HERRINGBONE**] 7837 Herschel Avenue, La Jolla, CA 92037, (858) 459-0221, www.herringboneeats.com

[**SEARSUCKER**] 611 Fifth Avenue, San Diego, CA 92101, (619) 233-7327, www.searsucker.com

[**SEARSUCKER**] 6900 East Camelback Road, Scottsdale, AZ 85251, www.searsucker.com/scottsdale

index

recipe index

recipes by main ingredient

[fish + seafoood]

[meat]

[poultry]

recipes by category

erringbon
LA JOLLA, CALIFORNIA
BURLAP
BARDINE
cker